Blessed Wrestling

BIBLICAL REFLECTIONS ON DISCERNING GOD'S CALL

Jessie Squires Colwell

First published in 2021 by the General Board of Higher Education and Ministry, Wesley's Foundery Books imprint, under ISBN 978-1-953052-50-6.

ISBN 978-1-791043-28-5

Copyright © 2021, 2026 by Abingdon Press. All rights reserved.

No part of this work may be reproduced or transmitted in any form or by any means, electronic or mechanical, including photocopying and recording, or by any information storage or retrieval system, except as may be expressly permitted by the 1976 Copyright Act, the 1998 Digital Millennium Copyright Act, or in writing from the publisher. Requests for permission can be addressed to Rights and Permissions, The United Methodist Publishing House, 810 12th Avenue South, Nashville TN 37203, or emailed to permissions@abingdonpress.com.

All web addresses were correct and operational at the time of publication.

Scripture quotations are from the New Revised Standard Version Bible, copyright © 1989 National Council of the Churches of Christ in the United States of America. Used by permission. All rights reserved worldwide.

Printed in the United States of America.

This book is dedicated to my youth pastor, Fran Givens, who saw God's calling upon my life before I was even aware it was happening. Thank you for challenging me and encouraging me to follow the direction of the Holy Spirit.

I also dedicate this book to all who are discerning. You are not alone; may you find a new direction forward as you wrestle with God.

Contents

Preface   vii

1. Wrestling with God: Jacob   1
2. Wrestling with Ourselves: Isaiah   19
3. Wrestling with Call: Mary   35
4. Wrestling with Identity: Paul   49
5. Wrestling with Others: Deborah   65
6. Wrestling with Detours: Esther   81
7. Wrestling with Obligation: Ruth   97
8. Wrestling with Letting Go: The Disciples   113

Afterword: Next Steps   129

Notes   131

Preface

WE RECOMMEND THAT you be continued for another year," the voice said to me from the other end of the line. My whole life had been building up to this moment, and these words were not the words I had longed to hear. The word *continued* usually has a positive connotation, and continuing something means you get to move forward. If you live in the world of The United Methodist Church, however, "continued" means you cannot go forward and must wait another year on the long journey to ordination.

In The United Methodist Church, by the time folks get to their ordination interview, they have already spent ten or more years preparing to meet with the Board of Ordained Ministry for this very important moment. To seek ordination in Virginia, candidates must earn a diploma from a four-year college, attend a three-year seminary, complete field and clinical pastoral education, and work in ministry for three years before they are even eligible to apply for full ordination. It is a grueling and faithful process.

Seven years ago, I went before the Board. I was ready; I was overprepared. After the meeting I walked to my car confidently, thinking that all my interviews had gone well. Then I received the call that, although I had passed two committees with flying colors, the Board decided to continue me for another year because I did not pass the third committee. When I asked why, my team leader said that, although I had not shared anything heretical during the oral interview, the committee thought my answers were too short. Therefore, the committee members concluded that they could not hear my theological voice and were not comfortable passing me.

In my effort not to talk too much, I had not talked enough. So I had to wait an additional year to interview again before the Board. Although this may not seem like a big deal, in my world it was the worst thing that had ever happened to me. I felt as though I had failed—publicly failed. I wondered, "How could this happen?" The church I was serving was flourishing under my leadership, but not passing this interview really made me question my effectiveness in ministry. My church grieved with me. I even questioned my call to ministry and had fleeting thoughts about applying for non-ministry jobs. I felt that the Board had inflicted a great injustice upon me.

In short, I was devastated. To make matters worse, during that year's annual conference, I sobbed as I watched twenty-five of my closest friends being ordained. I asked God, "Why them and not me?"

I wrestled with God over the Board's decision. I asked, "God, what else do you want from me? I have already given you my whole life." I wallowed for a while in my grief; I lay on the floor and cried. I ate some Ben and Jerry's. I shared with anyone who would listen how unfair my life seemed to be. By the grace of God, I had some wonderful people in my life who told me I would feel as if the world were ending but it really wasn't. I realized that what I saw as a roadblock to answering God's calling upon my life was simply another step I had to travel. I spent a lot of time that year wrestling with God and discerning.

The next year I passed the theology committee with flying colors and was ordained. What I learned in that year of growth was that it is okay and even beautiful to wrestle with God. I also became passionate about journeying alongside others as they were discerning. I started noticing that the work I was being asked to do in my life and ministry centered on discernment and calling. It has now become my

PREFACE

mission to encourage people to wrestle with God—especially in the difficult moments of life—because when we wrestle with God, we are changed and blessed.

I decided to write this book because I was unable to find the resource I wanted to give to others as they discerned God's call. Yes, there are other books about call that are helpful and good, but I wanted to write more specifically about the discernment process we all experience as we answer God's call. In these pages you will find the call stories of biblical people and people in my own life. They are all different, but my hope is that you will resonate with one of them. And yes, God still calls people to serve through the power and presence of the Holy Spirit.

Throughout my twelve years of ministry, I have wrestled with God, and I have been changed by the power of the Holy Spirit and the body of Christ. Last year I was named the chair of the same theology team that continued me so many years ago. On July 1, 2021, I became the director of clergy excellence for the Virginia Conference UMC and now have the awesome privilege and responsibility to watch over fifteen-hundred-plus clergy who continue to discern and answer God's calling upon their lives. Now it is my role to help equip the next generation of pastors. I have been blessed practicing this crazy thing we call ministry, and I have found my voice in helping others find theirs.

I am also blessed to help others know that throughout our lives we all continue to wrestle with God because this is how the Holy Spirit intertwines our will with God's will. We should not be afraid to wrestle with God, because when we do, like Jacob, we will be changed, blessed, and can walk toward a future with hope.

Blessed Wrestling is designed as an eight-week study. During this time, I invite you to learn from Jacob, Isaiah, Mary, Paul, Deborah, Esther, Ruth, and the disciples as they wrestled with God. Because of their encounters with God, they were changed and blessed to be a blessing—for us. Each week I invite you to spend time in prayer—listening, pondering, and even striving—as you discern what God is doing and wants to do in your life. Through this book, you will study call narratives from the Bible, participate either as an individual or in a group through reflective questions, listen to music, and have the opportunity to go even deeper into God's heart. Whether you are considering a call to ministry or mission or simply trying to figure out the next steps in life, my hope is that this book will be a tool of discernment and encouragement for you in whatever spiritual wrestling match you may find yourself.

Prayer

Wrestle with me, God, until I am molded more closely to your will than my own. Wrestle with me on the days I feel like giving up and on the days when I am full of myself. Wrestle with me in the yeses and noes of life. Wrestle with me over every decision I make and every word I say. Wrestle with me in my successes and my failures. Wrestle with me, for in your wrestling I hear the Holy Spirit. Wrestle with me until I am changed forever. Amen.

1
Wrestling with God
JACOB

The same night he got up and took his two wives, his two maids, and his eleven children, and crossed the ford of the Jabbok. He took them and sent them across the stream, and likewise everything that he had. Jacob was left alone; and a man wrestled with him until daybreak. When the man saw that he did not prevail against Jacob, he struck him on the hip socket; and Jacob's hip was put out of joint as he wrestled with him. Then he said, "Let me go, for the day is breaking." But Jacob said, "I will not let you go, unless you bless me." So he said to him, "What is your name?" And he said, "Jacob." Then the man said, "You shall no longer be called Jacob, but Israel, for you have striven with God and with humans, and have prevailed." Then Jacob asked him, "Please tell me your name." But he said, "Why is it that you ask my name?" And there he blessed him. So Jacob called the place Peniel, saying, "For I have seen God face to face, and yet my life is preserved." The sun rose upon him as he passed Penuel, limping because of his hip. Therefore to this day the Israelites do not eat the thigh muscle that is on the hip socket, because he struck Jacob on the hip socket at the thigh muscle. (Gen 32:22-32)

CHAPTER 1

WRESTLING WAS IN Jacob's very DNA. Even in the womb he wrestled with his brother, Esau, as he tried to be the first one born. As he was born, he clung to his brother's heel (Gen 25:26). Jacob's name means "trickster" and "supplanter." From birth he wanted more; and he did everything possible, including lie and deceive, to take away the gifts that belonged to Esau, who was the rightful firstborn son.

First, Jacob tricked Esau out of his birthright. Jacob took advantage of Esau when he was starving and vulnerable. Without thinking, Esau ended up trading his birthright, everything he was entitled to, for some soup—a hot lunch. Jacob then tricked his dying father, Isaac, into bestowing his blessing upon him. Gaining both the blessing and birthright meant that Esau now had to serve his younger brother for the rest of his life and lose his fair share of his father's inheritance. Due to Jacob's jealousy and manipulation, Esau lost everything and felt that he had no future (Gen 25:29-34; 27:1-40).

> How are you feeling as you read this story? Do you identify more with Jacob or Esau?

Esau was outraged and planned to kill Jacob after his father died. To preserve his life, the twins' mother, Rebekah, colluded with Jacob to flee for his life. But Genesis 32:22 tells us that the time of reckoning had arrived. Here we find Jacob the evening before he was to come face to face with the brother he had repeatedly betrayed. Esau was coming with a hoard of his men to settle accounts. It was time for payback. Would Jacob surrender, or would he fight for his life and for his family that he had sent on ahead?

Note the importance of the place where Jacob is waiting. He has been here before. Time and time again we realize that location is important and is in the Bible for a reason. Commentary tells us: "Just as God encountered Jacob when he fled the Promised Land because of his brother's anger, so also God now encounters him twenty years later at the point of reentry."[1]

Perhaps you are finding yourself at the place of reentry. Maybe you have taken a step back in life not knowing what your next steps should be. This scripture teaches us that this place of reentry is not a place to reside, but a place to pass through. Maybe you are reading this book because you feel stuck and unable to move forward. We all find ourselves stuck at some point in our lives. Yet God beckons us to move forward.

Jacob had a decision to make. He could return to where he had been hiding, or he could face his brother. God had called Jacob to this place of reentry. Jacob felt uneasy in his spirit because he realized his father-in-law was not happy with him, so he knew it was time to leave. But where would he go? Surely, he could not go home; that would not work out well for anyone. And where did God call Jacob to go? You guessed it. God told Jacob to go home. I am sure Jacob must have thought, "Anywhere but home, God." But God reassured him, as God tends to do, and said, "I will be with you" (31:3).

At this point of reentry there was no turning back. Jacob had already sent his family ahead of him. Surely his brother would not kill them but receive their presents as a peace offering. I wonder if he thought, "What should I do on my last night alive? Binge-watch Netflix or order a pizza?" He didn't even have time to decide on his favorite pizza topping, because the next thing he knew he was sneak-attacked by "a man" (32:24).

At first Jacob may have thought that the man was his brother Esau. Who else would come all that way to wrestle with him? It took Jacob a while to figure out who he was wrestling with. Over the course of the night he realized he was wrestling with God.[2] I think Jacob knew that he was wrestling with God because this was no ordinary opponent that he could defeat easily. He could not manipulate or lie himself out of this situation, skills he had used many times before.

The most interesting part about this scripture is that God initiated the wrestling match with Jacob. You may be asking, "Why would God want to initiate a wrestling match with Jacob, or us?

Isn't God the one who brings us peace?" That night, God initiated this wrestling match with Jacob so that Jacob would turn from his wayward path and experience reconciliation with his brother. God wrestles with our souls so that we, too, can find reconciliation with others and new life. Henceforth, Jacob would be going God's way, not his own way.

Hopes, Dreams, and Struggles

So often when life does not go our way, we turn to despair instead of hope; and yet in the Bible, time and time again we see that what people thought was the end was actually a new beginning. This has been true for my life as well. You see, I always thought I was on a certain path: go to college, start a career, marry, and have children. I was a very driven young woman, and most of the things I set my mind to I achieved. Along the way, things seemed to be going as planned. I enjoyed high school and leadership roles in my church. I got into the college I wanted and worked hard to get into my top choice of seminary. I became engaged to my high-school sweetheart, and everything seemed to be falling into place. My life was coming true, just as I had always dreamed it would.

> What has been the trajectory of your life? What dreams do you have? Where does God play in?

My calling to ordained ministry ended the path of this trajectory—this life that I had planned for myself. When I left college I was engaged to my high-school sweetheart. In a grand romantic gesture of lighting up an island in the middle of a lake, he had asked me to marry him on Christmas Eve of my senior year of college while he was a junior. I think he thought that if he asked me to marry him, I would not go to seminary. But I was called by God, and I had worked so hard to get into Duke Divinity School.

I went to Duke, and we tried to make our long-distance relationship work; but something had changed in our relationship, and we both decided that the best thing for us to do would be to call off our engagement and go our separate ways. Even though I was excited to pursue God's calling on my life, this new season of life was not without grief. In fact, I thought my life was over. The life I had envisioned had evaporated into thin air. Five years of building a relationship and a life with the man I loved were gone. What was I supposed to do now?

> What is a big decision that you've made? Have you ever had to start over?

You may be able to relate to a moment like this. These are the moments that define us: we have a choice to remain stuck in uncertainty or move forward into the future with the hope that God promises to us through our faith. If only I had known then what God had in store for me—that after seminary and in my first church God would bring a new man into my life—my now husband, who supported my call to ministry and rejoiced in who God created me to be. If only I had known then that we would be blessed with an incredible son. If only I had known all the amazing people whom God would place in my life to bring me through tough times and offer me encouragement and affirmation. If only I had known how different my life would turn out and how it would be so much better than I ever could have imagined in that moment, perhaps I would not have had such a tough spiritual wrestling match with God. It was in this season of grief in my life that I was blessed to wrestle with God and where God formed me into the person I am and sent me forward with hope.

All those years ago in my first year of seminary, it was undeniable that God had called me to ministry. I finally realized that God had set me on a new trajectory. However, my type A self was uncomfortable because I did not know where this trajectory would take me. Surprisingly, I was open to this new path and had the assurance that

CHAPTER 1

even though I didn't know where I was going, God was leading me to the place where I was supposed to be.

During that first year of seminary I wrestled with God a lot. I kept questioning my decision to pursue ministry. I asked myself many questions that you may be thinking about right now. Was I cut out for the ups and downs of ministry? Was my faith strong enough? Was I smart enough to retain my scriptural and theological foundation? How would I handle a crisis? Could I really make a difference for the kingdom of God? And the answer to all these questions was simple: But God . . .

> What questions are you asking God? What are your struggles?

But God . . .

One of the things I love the most about Scripture is how many times a sentence includes "but God . . ." This is our story as Christians. When Jesus ascended to heaven, the disciples wondered, "Now what?" And God gave the gift of the Holy Spirit. God continues to usher in new life, despite our shortcomings. We mind our own business, we get ourselves in trouble, but God . . . shows up. We think all hope is lost and Jesus is dead to us, but God . . .

For me, like many others, my "but God" experience is that I realized I could do nothing without God's help, especially answer God's call. After all, God was the one who called me in the first place, and God continues to be the one to carry me through this journey of ministry. I have had many "but God" moments throughout my life because I have spent much of my life wrestling with God. Sound familiar to you?

Wrestling with God

My first experience wrestling with God happened when I was sixteen years old on a mission trip to help rebuild a church burned down by the Ku Klux Klan in Gadsden, South Carolina. This was the first time in my young life that I had witnessed embodied racism. What left the greatest impression on me during that mission trip was that we were invited to stay in the homes of church members while we were there. These church members, who had lost their church because of someone who looked like me, allowed strangers to come and stay in their houses so that together we could rebuild their house of worship. And it was there amidst the ashes that God wrestled with me, blessed me, and called me to a new life.

> When have you experienced God's love?

My new life was different from before. Honestly it was harder, but harder in a good way because I now had a purpose. Before, I felt as though I were floating around aimlessly. In this moment of answering God's calling upon my life, I finally felt at peace. I voiced my calling to be a pastor to my youth group and the congregation whose church had been burned down. In that moment, like Jacob, my life was changed forever.

Beauty from Ashes

The beautiful thing about the God we serve is that God calls all of us to service. Through the sacrament of baptism, we are claimed by God and sent out by the Holy Spirit to do God's work. We are all made in God's image, and we uniquely reflect God's image through the way we live out our gifts in the world. In the book of Ephesians, the apostle Paul shares that some are called to preach, some are called to be teachers, and some are called to be evangelists. We are all called to do something with our gifts that builds up the body of Christ (4:11-16). Sometimes it takes us a while to figure out what our gifts are and how we should be using them. What we do know is that God always brings life out of death; and when we use our gifts for God's glory, we, too, will be part of the ministry of bringing new life to the world.

All through the Bible, God takes agents of death and turns them into signs of life. Take ashes for instance. In the Old Testament, ashes were used as a symbol of mourning. They were routinely discarded after the priests had burned sacrifices. But there is also something very interesting about ashes. When mixed with spring water, they were used to cleanse those deemed ritually impure (Num 19:9-10). These very ashes that were cast aside as trash, as not needed, were the elements used to invite people back into God's family. This is the kind of God we serve, a God who takes a mark of death and turns it into new life.

In the ashes of a church that had been burned down due to racism and hatred, a call was born into my life, and I found new life and new purpose through answering God's call. So today, if you find yourself steeped in the sackcloth and ashes of life, for whatever reason, do not fear the death of your life as you know it. Be open for certain parts of your life to die so that other parts may be born anew.

Discernment is about letting life as we know it die so that we can pursue God's will—God's preferred future for us—rather than our own way. That is what makes it so hard. It is not fun to wrestle with God, yet that is exactly what God calls us to do because, through this time of wrestling, we will come out on the other side knowing more clearly what God has called us to do. So don't be afraid to wrestle with God; in fact, I highly recommend it! By wrestling and engaging with God we can find our next steps forward.

Called to Something Greater

Wrestling with God is not something you can do by yourself. We are invited to discern God's calling upon our lives with the help of God and the community of God. That is the good news: God's calling upon our lives is confirmed by the Holy Spirit and in community. Like Jacob, we all wrestle with God. We wrestle because we want answers to the big questions of life. We desire direction. We want to be more attuned to God's will. Wrestling with God is not something to be ashamed of. In fact, wrestling with God embodies our desire to know God. When we wrestle with God, we acknowledge that God is already working in our lives, calling us to respond, be more, dream bigger, help bring in God's kingdom, and do it God's way.

Many situations in our lives cause us to wrestle with God. Usually we find ourselves wrestling with God over important decisions. Maybe you find yourself wrestling with God over something unexpected that has happened in your life. Perhaps you are wrestling with God and questioning God's goodness after you have experienced the death of a loved one or the loss of an important relationship. Maybe you are wrestling with God over the state of the world. We have all witnessed poverty, systemic racial injustice, hatred, violence, and even apathy when it comes to loving our neighbors. We grieve these inequalities and carry our own personal grief with us, yet God calls us to be a part of something bigger than ourselves so we can help others and bring hope to a world that is so often in darkness. There are many reasons we find ourselves in a spiritual wrestling match with God, but the good news is that God meets us there, willing to listen and willing to engage us as God gives us a new way forward.

We wrestle with God when we find ourselves at a breaking point. Jacob was at his breaking point. His older brother was coming for him because he had stolen his brother's blessing and birthright, and Jacob probably thought his life was over. We find him alone with his thoughts . . . preparing for his eminent death. But in his trial, Jacob accepted that God had another way for him and his descendants (Gen 27:41-42).[3]

God is our Creator and Giver of life, and it is God who continues to initiate a relationship with us through the power and presence of the Holy Spirit. God is always speaking to our hearts, but are we listening? More important, are we responding? The moment we profess Jesus Christ with our lips, the Holy Spirit enters our hearts. God is no longer whispering from the outside but speaking to us on the inside. This is where our wrestling match with God originates. Anytime we think, say, or do anything contrary to God's will, the Holy Spirit wrestles with our souls. God wrestles with us because God cares about us. God is not content for us to settle being less than who we were created to be. God continues to pursue us and offer us grace, mercy, and forgiveness. So, like Jacob, we are called to wrestle with God.

> What part of Jacob's story speaks to you? Reflecting on the rest of the story, how did this encounter change Jacob? What does it mean that Jacob's new name, Israel, became the name of a nation?

Cling to God

Wrestling with God may seem counterintuitive. Why would we want to wrestle with God? God is the Almighty; and, of course, God will always win. In the wrestling we realize that we do not wrestle with God to win. We wrestle with God to understand more clearly where God is leading us next. We wrestle with God because this is a way for us to cling to God so that we will know God more deeply. We wrestle with God because God never gives up on us, so we should never give up on God.

Surprisingly, in this scripture, even after Jacob realized he was wrestling with God, he did not give up. What is beautiful about this scripture is that Jacob fought back. This is a part of our story as the people of God: we are not afraid to engage with God, even when things get tough. Adam and Eve were cast out of the garden because of their sin, but they continued to live and strove to follow God (Gen 3:23). The Israelites spent forty years in the wilderness, but they did not give up on the hope of the Promised Land. Noah and his family spent forty days at sea not knowing if they would ever see land again, but they persevered. The disciples waited fifty days for the coming of the Holy Spirit (Acts 2:1).[4] Then Pentecost happened, and they were led forward by the power of the Holy Spirit.

Jesus Christ made it possible for us to continue to press on because we have hope in eternal life, our new Promised Land. As the people of God, we are called to respond to God's call, God's initiation upon our lives. Wrestling with God is a faithful response to God's call. Wrestling is not a burden or a punishment; it is God's way of getting our attention and leading us forward into the people God has created us to be.

At this moment, Jacob had a decision to make. He could give up and allow the "man" to defeat him. Surely certain death awaited him with his brother in the morning anyway. Yet, there was something in Jacob that told him not to give up but to fight for his life. Just as he had hung on to the heel of his brother at birth, here Jacob would not let go of God. He wrestled with God all night (Gen 32:22-26).

Jacob took a great risk. The Bible tells us that God did not allow God's people to see the face of God or they would perish. Daylight was approaching, and both Jacob and God knew that Jacob could die if he saw God's face in the light of the new day. God told Jacob to let go to preserve Jacob's life.

> What risks are you taking if you don't engage with God? How are you clinging to God now?

Answering God's call upon our lives requires risk. It is risky because we are going into the unknown. It is risky because we must surrender everything. It is risky because it requires great sacrifice. Yet, without risk, there is no blessing.

As you continue to answer God's call upon your life, I encourage you to talk to a missionary. Talk about risk. Missionaries are people who literally say, "Send me" and leave the rest up to God. I have been blessed in my life to encounter many missionaries who have

CHAPTER 1

now become my friends. It is interesting to me that they all have one thing in common: an openness to be among God's people wherever there is a need.

Recently I was talking with my friend, missionary and pastor Rev. Nancy Robinson. She shared with me that she has done a lot of training with churches on how to be in mission. She said, "You are a missionary when you are participating in God's work and when your life speaks of your inward faith." Nancy is one of those people who can feel at home anywhere because the people of God are her earthly home. She has been all over the world serving God's people, and she is passionate in sparking the passion of mission in others. She has taken great risks as she has put her life on hold in order to go to places she had never been before.

Nancy shared with me about a time when she wrestled with God. She had grown up in Zimbabwe as a child of two missionaries. She had to leave quite suddenly in her youth when she and her family were deported by the white colonial government. She never really got to say goodbye or find closure. That was until one day her pastor asked if she was interested in going on a mission trip to Zimbabwe. Immediately Nancy was interested, but she thought, "There is no way I can go." Family obligation and the cost of the trip kept her from saying yes. Then a woman in her congregation handed her a personal check for three thousand dollars, and she was out of excuses.

Nancy went on that mission trip, and once her feet hit the ground in Zimbabwe, she felt a deep sense of peace. This experience triggered a catharsis of healing and spiritual focus as she heard clearly God's call to mission. It was there that she recognized she had gifts for this calling. Since that time Nancy has gone all over the world. She has wrestled with God since that day, but the wrestling has taken a different form. Now when she wrestles with God, it is God calling her to something new. Nancy currently serves as a deacon and the lead pastor of a church in Richmond, Virginia. There she uses her gifts for mission with her congregation, but Nancy continues to be open to wherever God will send her next. In her wrestling with God, Nancy has found hope. In taking risks for the glory of God, Nancy has found a blessing.

When Jacob wrestled with God, he clung to God because Jacob needed something from God. Jacob risked his own life because he needed a blessing. Call it a last resort, but Jacob did believe that God could save him from the wrath of his brother. This blessing he was fighting for was different than the blessing he had stolen from his brother. This blessing could not be gained by deceit or manipulation; it was given by God as a gift. In God's action of granting Jacob a blessing, Jacob's life was preserved.

God not only spared Jacob's life, but through God's blessing Jacob received a new name and a new identity. God named him "Israel," which means "strives with God" (Gen 32:28) or "God-wrestler" as I like to call him. What did Jacob have to be afraid of? His name was "God-wrestler"! Surely his brother would not kill him now.

God's blessing did not come without a cost. Before the fight ended, God struck Jacob in the hip socket, damaging his hip for life. The way Jacob walked was changed forever, but he was blessed to live another day. His limp was a badge of honor and a constant reminder of who he was and who God is. This interaction with God also affected the whole community. From that day forward they did not eat the meat of animal at the hip socket (vv. 31-32). Jacob was not the only one changed by this wrestling match. The community of God was changed as well.

God's calling upon our lives changes us. It refines us; it gives us strength, endurance, and a new identity. All we need to do is be willing to follow where God is calling us to go. Like Jacob, may we not be afraid to be changed so that others may come to know the God of grace and mercy that we serve.

Jacob went on from this moment, and instead of heading into certain death, he walked into the open arms of his brother, Esau. This scene of forgiveness and reconciliation is much like the gospel lesson in Luke 15 on the prodigal son. During the many years Jacob was in hiding, Esau had made a life for himself. He had gained power and prestige, as evidenced by the entourage he had with him. He could have been an agent of death that day when he encountered the brother who betrayed him. Instead, he chose to forgive Jacob and welcome his family into his own (Gen 33). That day, at the point of reentry, this family started a new life together and began to move forward from a past filled with pain.

Blessed to Be a Blessing

Like his ancestor Abraham, Jacob and his descendants were blessed so they could be a blessing. The amazing thing about answering God's calling upon our lives is that it does not affect only us. Answering God's call can save other people's lives literally, figuratively, and spiritually. One way I have felt my call affirmed is when God continues to place me in other people's lives, especially when they need someone to talk to. This has happened to me when shopping in the supermarket, jogging in my neighborhood, or minding my own business in a coffee shop. You never know all the ways in which God will use your life to serve others, but one thing is certain: when we live into God's calling upon our lives, we can have a greater impact on the world.

At my first pastoral appointment there was a woman named Peggy who often asked if I had time to talk to discuss faith matters. So I made time to spend with Peggy to see what was on her mind and heart. I could tell she was wrestling with God regarding a call to ministry that was evident to me, but not yet evident to her. Peggy and I spent many a night at the local pizza shop discussing deep theological questions and ways to help the church.

At the time, I asked Peggy if she thought she was called to ministry. She laughed in my face and said, "No!" But she happened to have a heart for social justice, she happened to be gifted at preaching, and she happened to be passionate about worship. After I went to my next appointment, Peggy contacted me and shared that she had started the process to become a pastor. I was ecstatic that she was answering God's call and that she had amazing pastors to journey with during her discernment.

Today I celebrate that Peggy listened to the Holy Spirit and that so many people have been impacted by all the ways she embodies the good news of Jesus Christ. Peggy and I still talk, especially when one of us is wrestling with God. God continues to wrestle with each one of us as we listen to the Holy Spirit at work in our lives.

This Week

After rereading Jacob's story, take some time to meditate upon this thought by the theologian St. Augustine. In his *Confessions*, Augustine wrote: "Thou hast made us for thyself and restless is our heart until it comes to rest in thee."[5] How does your soul resound with this statement: God creates a restlessness in our hearts for a reason, so that we will engage God's grace, love, and power. May we attend to God's call without fear, without hesitation, but with conviction, purpose, passion, and our entire self.

Wrestling with God Spotlight: Hannah Hanson

I first met Hannah in New York City at a board meeting. We had a lot in common. We were both young women from Virginia who were passionate about mission. I had gone the local ministry route, while Hannah traveled the world. In high school Hannah felt God calling her to serve. At her home church, her pastor and congregation members affirmed this call in her. Looking back, Hannah acknowledged that she knew she was called but that she did not know what she would end up doing. All she knew is that she was passionate about mission and justice. In her first mission position, she served in South Africa.

Hannah shared with me that she really wrestled with God during that time. She had a vision for how she wanted things to go, but due to circumstances beyond her control, she had to leave her current

CHAPTER 1

location and go to the next place where God was calling her to serve. Hannah grieved leaving the community who had become family. As she reflected on that time of wrestling with God, she later found peace when she realized that we may not always have the answers we want from God in the moment but that God's abiding peace comes from learning how to ask better questions.

Hannah now works as the director of young adult mission service for Global Ministries, and she journeys alongside young adults who are discerning how God is calling them to serve. She encourages them to continue to ask questions, and she tells them: "There is not only one path. There is not just one right answer." She encourages them to try the thing they feel God calling them to do next and to know that God will take care of the rest. I am so thankful for Hannah's faithful witness and how a new generation is benefiting from her passion for discernment and mission.

―――――

God has created each of us with unique gifts and abilities to do God's holy work. As you read through this study, be open to all the different ways God can use you to serve. Perhaps you can keep the job you have and continue to do God's ministry, or maybe God is calling you in a completely different way. Maybe God is calling you to go on a mission trip to see if your heart may be awakened to the call of mission. Be open to the guidance of the Holy Spirit as God wrestles with you over which way you should go.

Answering God's calling upon your life is not for the faint of heart. It can require long days, sleepless nights, sweat, tears, and deep loss. And yet wrestling with God is beautiful; it is life-giving; it is authentic; it matters; and it is what we have been called to do as the people of God. Whether you have been called to mission, ordained ministry, or something else, God has a purpose for your life. Like Jacob, may we choose to wrestle with God so that we are changed, blessed, and sent forward with hope!

PRAY

Wrestle with me, God, when I won't stop fighting you. Wrestle with me when I won't let go until I feel blessed. Wrestle with me on the days I am not willing to surrender to your will. Wrestle with me when I question my calling and purpose. Wrestle with me when all I can see is death and not life. Remind me that new life is right around the corner and that my identity comes from you and not the world. Help me to discern your voice among the many voices fighting for my attention and time. Help me to be changed forever. Amen.

REFLECT

1. What would it be like for you to wrestle with God?
2. What are your "but God" moments?
3. How would you like God to bless you?
4. How was Jacob changed forever due to his experience? Are there ways you are looking to change?
5. How do Augustine's words resound in your soul?

LISTEN

"Jacob's Song" by Briana Babineaux
https://www.youtube.com/watch?v=GyxZcISJ-2o

JOURNAL

Keep a record of your prayer requests, answers to prayers, and your "but God" moments.

2
Wrestling with Ourselves
ISAIAH

In the year that King Uzziah died, I saw the Lord sitting on a throne, high and lofty; and the hem of his robe filled the temple. Seraphs were in attendance above him; each had six wings: with two they covered their faces, and with two they covered their feet, and with two they flew. And one called to another and said:

> "Holy, holy, holy is the LORD of hosts;
> the whole earth is full of his glory."

The pivots on the thresholds shook at the voices of those who called, and the house filled with smoke. And I said: "Woe is me! I am lost, for I am a man of unclean lips, and I live among a people of unclean lips; yet my eyes have seen the King, the LORD of hosts!"

Then one of the seraphs flew to me, holding a live coal that had been taken from the altar with a pair of tongs. The seraph touched my mouth with it and said: "Now that this has touched your lips, your guilt has departed and your sin is blotted out." Then I heard the voice of the Lord saying, "Whom shall I send, and who will go for us?" And I said, "Here am I; send me!" (Isa 6:1-8)

CHAPTER 2

THE PROPHET ISAIAH shows it is possible to have an internal wrestling match as we answer God's call. The book that bears his name begins with Isaiah pronouncing judgment against God's people.[1] It is interesting that Isaiah starts this work before God calls him to serve. In this moment in Isaiah 6, Isaiah's life is changed forever. His life is no longer about him but about what God is calling him to do. There are several things happening in the moment Isaiah decides to say yes to God. First, he had an amazing vision of God. What a gift! Isaiah's vision is how many of us think about God today. God is almighty; God is too big for us to even fathom or imagine. God is mysterious, and we will never be able to fully realize God's greatness and majesty.

I often wonder how Isaiah felt when he experienced this vision. Was he scared? Was he excited? Could he even contain himself? These are the very same feelings so many people have when God is calling them to serve. Like Isaiah, many times we do not feel worthy. Isaiah's excuse was that he was sinful and therefore was not fit for service to God. How could he serve a perfect God when he knew he was not perfect? How could God cleanse him when he knew he was going to get dirty again? Many times, in the life of our faith, we ask God these questions. Like Isaiah, we also make excuses for why we feel unfit to serve God.

The Past, Our Greatest Teacher

Sometimes we may feel that we are disqualified from answering God's call because of our past. We may feel guilty about things we have done or said, and we may feel that because of these mistakes we have made, we are not fit to serve God in a new way. We wrestle with ourselves over the past, but the danger in wrestling with ourselves in this way is that we get stuck in the past and are unable to see God's present and future for our lives.

We all have a past. We all have things we look back on and wish we could do differently. It is okay to wrestle with ourselves through these events if we learn from them and use what we have learned about ourselves to honor God with our lives. Remember, God called people who had a past. Jacob was a manipulator, Moses was a murderer, David was an adulterer. Paul was a conspirator, and Peter was a traitor. Yet through their faith in God, they found redemption and a place to serve God. Through repentance and trust in God, they were cleansed of their sins and continued to serve God.

A Clean and Right Spirit Within

As a response to Isaiah's excuse, God orchestrated a cleansing for Isaiah. As the HarperCollins Study Bible puts it: When Isaiah is "cleansed by the burning coal from the altar, Isaiah may now speak for God."[2] This moment for Isaiah reminds us that when we are called by God, we, too, are called to interpret God's Word to others. We, too, are called to speak on behalf of God, and that is an awesome responsibility.

To answer God's call, we, too, must be cleansed by God—set apart so we can help others experience God. To speak on behalf of God, our hearts and intentions must remain pure—impossible without God's grace. Our words must be scripturally supported to express the fundamental tenor of the entire Bible. Our own agendas must be swept aside, and we must continue to focus our minds and hearts on Christ. To answer God's call, many cobwebs must be swept out of our hearts.

We first take part in God's cleansing by acknowledging who we are. We are sinners in need of God's grace. When we claim who we are in light of our relationship with Jesus Christ, God takes the identity created for us by ourselves and the world, and refashions our identity into the image that God has created within us. Being open to God's cleansing of our souls is vital to lifelong ministry. We are sinners, but Romans 3:24 reminds us we are "justified by [Christ's] grace as a gift, through the redemption that is in Christ Jesus."

CHAPTER 2

So, how can be we cleansed? In one word: repentance. Through repentance we express our genuine apology for the sins we have committed. In the act of repentance, we surrender our lives to God. We turn away from our sins and turn toward God, and God cleanses our souls and helps refocus our minds and hearts on God's will. But this is not a one-time event. In fact, we are called to surrender our lives to God every day. In the moment Isaiah's lips were cleansed, so was his soul. After that moment, his word testified to the words of God and not his own. Answering God's call means that we, too, will weigh carefully every word we say so that our words can be used for God's glory.

I find it interesting that at no time does Isaiah say, "Wait a minute, seraph; please do not put that hot coal on my lips. Is there another way we can do this purifying ritual?" Without any protest from Isaiah, the seraph touches Isaiah's lips with the live coal, and he is cleansed of his sin. Since this was a vision, we hope that Isaiah was not burned from this encounter. Instead, through this encounter with God, Isaiah found the confidence to answer God's call.

Isaiah is not the only person who was charged to carry the word of God through his lips. In the story of Ezekiel's call, through a vision he is instructed to eat a scroll and then go talk to the Israelites. "He said to me, 'O mortal, eat what is offered to you; eat this scroll, and go, speak to the house of Israel.' So I opened my mouth, and he gave me the scroll to eat. He said to me, 'Mortal, eat this scroll that I give you and fill your stomach with it.' Then I ate it; and in my mouth it was as sweet as honey" (Ezek 3:1-3). After Ezekiel eats the scroll, the word of God is within him. He becomes the embodied word of God to God's people.

Isaiah's lips were touched with a red-hot coal; and Ezekiel, through his lips, ate the scroll containing the word of God. Likewise, we are called to carry the good news of the Bible on our lips. We can do this through spending time each day studying God's Word—the Bible—both the Old and New Testaments. We can also understand God's Word and will in a deeper way as we participate in the sacraments of the church.

I am glad that baptism is our symbolic cleansing ritual; no more hot coals or eating papyrus! Through words of repentance, God cleanses our sins, and through the waters of baptism, we announce to the world that our cleansing has taken place. Through the liturgy of Holy Communion, we corporately confess our sins to God, repent, and receive God's grace. Through this beautiful liturgy, we are reminded that God calls us from the waters of baptism to bring living water to the world. You may wonder, "Does God even need us? Why would God call us to serve?"

The answer is because God loves us. In the book *Acts: Catching Up with the Spirit* by Matt Skinner, we hear these words of assurance and encouragement. Skinner says, "The church . . . is [how] Jesus remains active in the world."[3] The beautiful thing about the birth of the church on Pentecost is that we now get to participate in God's ministry in the world. Through our baptism, we are called to discipleship and service. God has placed a calling on all our lives, but it is up to us to discern further exactly what God is calling us to do. We must not get stuck wrestling with ourselves and living in the past or being paralyzed in the present.

Instead of being filled with joy and excitement, so often we find ourselves fearful and questioning God's call. We ask God, "Are you really calling me? Are you sure you didn't mean to call that person over there?" Looking through the Bible, we see that we are not alone. Many people called by God did not think they could rise to the occasion. For instance, when God called Moses from the burning bush, Moses replied, "Who am I that I should go to Pharaoh, and bring the Israelites out of Egypt?" (Exod 3:11). When Gideon was called to serve, he responded, "How I can deliver Israel?" (Judg 6:15). It seems that both Moses and Gideon had a case of imposter syndrome. Each found himself to be in opposition to the man he thought he was and to the man God was calling him to be.

CHAPTER 2

Imposter Syndrome

Through this scripture, we can intuit that Isaiah experienced imposter syndrome. He could not understand why God was calling him, a "man of unclean lips" (Isa 6:5), to be part of God's ministry in the world. Isaiah could not rectify his sinful nature with his calling. Left to his own devices, he might have felt defeated because of his sin and turned away from God's calling upon his life. In this scripture Isaiah names the root of imposter syndrome: our desire to serve God and our human struggle with sin.

The apostle Paul names this same struggle:

> I do not understand my own actions. For I do not do what I want, but I do the very thing I hate. Now if I do what I do not want, I agree that the law is good. But in fact it is no longer I that do it, but sin that dwells within me. For I know that nothing good dwells within me, that is, in my flesh. I can will what is right, but I cannot do it. For I do not do the good I want, but the evil I do not want is what I do. Now if I do what I do not want, it is no longer I that do it, but sin that dwells within me. (Rom 7:15-20)

Paul was clearly called by God on the road to Damascus, and yet he questioned his ability to serve. We, too, may struggle with our own sin. We wonder, "How are we supposed to serve God when we are imperfect due to our sinful nature?" Yet God calls us to serve anyway. Though we are imperfect, God perfectly loves us and equips us to serve through our faith in Jesus Christ and the power of the Holy Spirit.

> Have you ever felt like an imposter? What did you do or not do?

Am I Worthy? Am I Enough?

As you continue your journey of discernment, you may experience times when you question yourself and God. You may experience times when you wrestle with your own leadership or it is questioned by others. This is normal. It does not necessarily mean that God has not called you, but these thoughts and feelings of doubt are something that you must name and work through with God and the supportive community of God's people.

> What doubts do you have? About yourself? Your future?

Sometimes, imposter syndrome can be more subtle. It can be seen in the way we doubt ourselves, even when we know that God will make a way for us to answer God's call. It can be seen when we keep rewriting a sermon or question our interactions with those we are leading. It can be seen in the way we compare ourselves to others. Like Isaiah, we, too, make excuses for why we are unable to serve God. But, throughout the Bible, we see that God called imperfect people to share God's perfect love.

Maybe you have experienced imposter syndrome. In fact, maybe that is why you are reading this book to discern further if God is really calling you. Have you ever been in a situation and you just felt that you did not belong, even though you could not explain why? Sometimes these thoughts arise from doubting ourselves. We can be our own worst critic. Sometimes these feelings arise because of the way others treat us. Whatever the reason, I think at some point we have all felt like an imposter.

> Think of a time when you felt you didn't belong or when someone you know felt they didn't belong. What was it like?

CHAPTER 2

Our culture of comparison feeds imposter syndrome. Scrolling through feeds we compare ourselves to other people's lives. We yearn for people to love us publicly even if we have no close personal relationship with them privately. Since people typically share the best of themselves, we compare ourselves to a standard that is unattainable. Even though I believe there are some positives to social media, such as staying connected, I also believe this technology has planted within each of us deep-seated doubt that did not exist before. The danger of the constant comparison of social media is that we can lose our own identity as we try to adhere to an unrealistic standard. In so doing, we can lose sight of who God is calling us to be.

> How does social media contribute to imposter syndrome?

Why do we compare ourselves to others? It is in our human DNA to do so. After all, the first death in Scripture, the death of Abel, happened because Cain was jealous (Gen 4:1-16). He could not stand being second best. We compare ourselves and our calls with others too. We hear someone's call story and think, "Wow! Nothing like that has even happened to me, so I must not be called."

I hope you find in these pages that all our call stories are different yet valid. No one story looks exactly like another. Our calls are different because we serve a multifaceted God who loves diversity. We are all called to do different things to build up the body of Christ. So please, beloved child of God, take heart when the voices in your head get you down; the Holy Spirit will continue to call you forward and bless you to serve.

When we buy into imposter syndrome, we get in our own way and rob others of experiencing our God-given gifts. I talked to a good friend on the phone the other day. Chelsea and I do not talk often, but when we do, the Holy Spirit shows up. On this day Chelsea shared how she was wrestling with the decision to move forward in the next step to ordained ministry. I knew that she could finish all the work required; but I also knew that, with all her other responsibilities, she would be running herself into the ground to complete it on time and up to her own standards. After a while, Chelsea admitted that the pressure to move forward so quickly had come from comparing herself to others. When she took a step back, she saw that she was in ministry where she was. I had the joy that day to remind Chelsea who I knew her to be and name her many gifts for ministry. We both walked away from the conversation feeling uplifted. This conversation reminded me that it is so easy to fall into the trap of comparing ourselves to others, and we need our friends to affirm our gifts and encourage us so that we can continue to answer God's call.

> When was the last time you experienced the presence of God? What is it like to experience God in your life?

In my twelve years of ministry, I have realized that imposter syndrome is not just a rite of passage you experience in seminary; it is something that can crop up throughout your life, even if you are exactly where God is calling you be. Imposter syndrome happens because in our humanity we wonder, "Why would God call me to serve?" We, like Isaiah, cannot understand why God would call even us to serve. And yet, God calls us anyway. Instead of spending priceless time and energy wrestling with yourself, trust in God's call upon your life. Continue to discern God's call by seeking out opportunities that are life-giving.

Words of Life and Death

I believe that it is no mistake that Isaiah's lips were purified, because it is through our lips that we can choose to speak words of death or words of life. Word of death are words people speak upon us that cause us to doubt ourselves and cause us to question God. In her book *Be Bold: Finding Your Fierce*, Rev. Rachel Billups describes words of death that were spoken over her when she was a young girl; she calls these words a "limitation prophecy."[4] She describes a limitation prophecy as spoken words that "limit your view of yourself and the world around you."[5] The danger of limitation prophecies is that sometimes we believe them.

Sometimes we take the opinion of one person and let that person dictate our next steps in life. This is where our spiritual wrestling match originates within us. We continue to ask ourselves who we are, what are our gifts, and what is God calling us to do? No one can answer that for us. To move forward we must find affirmation from the Holy Spirit and the body of Christ.

> When was a time that someone put unreasonable limits on you?

This past week I celebrated a beautiful milestone in the life of one of my friends, Martha Stokes, as she was elected to serve as our conference lay leader. This means she is the conduit for congregations in our conference. She will be the main source of communication on everything happening in our conference, and she has been charged to care for thousands of people.

Martha thought this moment would never happen for her. At a young age she voiced a call to ministry, but one voice rose above the rest and did not affirm her call. So she vowed to continue to serve God at the local congregation level. She found a passion for ministry to people with disabilities and those who were the most vulnerable. Martha continued to find affirmation in her gifts from the Holy Spirit, and over her many years of service, she has found affirmation from the body of Christ. Her advice to those discerning is this: "Do not let one voice be the guiding factor in answering God's call. Let people see your gifts and your passion. Reach out and ask for people to support you. You never know where it might lead you."

Keeping the Focus on God

Many cautionary tales in the Bible remind us to listen to God's words and not the words of others who do not have our best interests in mind. This is how Adam and Eve got into trouble; they believed the words of someone else over God's truth. Everything was going fine in the garden for Adam and Eve until the serpent (the devil) put doubt in Eve's mind about what she had been called to do. With the words, "You will not die" from the serpent, Eve turned away from God and toward the serpent with disastrous results for all of us (Gen 3:4).

Why is it that we, too, believe these words of death even when we know they are lies? In our humanity we question everything, even ourselves, and even God's goodness. But God continues to call after us, "Where are you?" (v. 9). Even when we experience words of death or find ourselves feeling dead spiritually, God continues to pursue us and is ready to offer us renewal.

I am hopeful that we can all think of a time when someone spoke a blessing upon us or some amazing words of encouragement. Words of life are the words we hear from others who speak blessing upon our lives. These are the people who believe in us, who see what we are capable of and rejoice when we use our gifts to God's glory. Words of life are the things we say to ourselves that give us confidence that we are becoming the people God has called us to be.

These clarifying moments in our lives are the moments when everything seems to make sense, and we realize God has been leading us somewhere all along. I was blessed to have an amazing youth pastor and other pastors who spoke words of life over me, people who recognized God's gifts within me and then encouraged me to discern further where God was calling me to go. I often wonder where I would be today without these people who spoke life over me.

So, where would God find you today if God came looking for you? Would God find someone who believes God's words of life or society's words of death? Maybe you have experienced people in your life who were not supportive when you voiced a call to serve God. Yet, when God calls us to serve, we, too, are called to respond as Isaiah did: "Here am I; send me!" (Isa 6:8).

Instead of being our own biggest critic, we need to become our own biggest fan. Why? Because we are made in the image of God, and that statement in itself (Gen 2) shows us that we already have worth because of who God is. We have, as United Methodists like to say, "sacred worth,"[6] yet we also must own that we are sinners.

We make mistakes, but we are still called to serve God through Christ, who makes us righteous through our faith. So we can think of ourselves highly, not out of arrogance or pride, but because of God who knows what we are capable of even when we do not.

As you read this chapter, I want you to think about this: Has there ever been a time in your life when someone else asked you if you were interested in ministry? Or has someone ever acknowledged your gifts for teaching, love of mission, or passion for justice? These instances are other people who recognize God working in you, who recognize your gifts and sacred worth. These people recognize God in you. So, take heart; do not get sidetracked by imposter syndrome or limitation prophecies, but keep your ears alert for how God is calling you to move forward with words of life.

Wrestling with Ourselves Spotlight: Rev. Ashley Anne Sipe

In seminary I became best friends with a young woman named Ashley who had experienced a limitation prophecy spoken over her life. She had grown up in a faith tradition that did not support women in ministry and would never allow them to preach. She shared this with me and told me this is why she would not be pursuing ordained ministry, because for her she thought it was impossible.

But Ashley is a powerful preacher. We were in the same preaching class, and when I heard her preach, I witnessed the good news of Jesus Christ being embodied in her words of life. It was so strange and amazing to see my best friend, whom I saw every day, in this new light as a prophet. When I shared with her that I thought her sermon was powerful, she thanked me but seemed sad.

Ashley believed the words of death and limitation prophecy that had been spoken over her life. Like Isaiah, Ashley did not think she was good enough to fulfill God's calling upon her life. For Ashley, this feeling did not come from her lack of knowledge or gifts; it came from her situation in life—that she happened to be a woman. When Ashley preached she felt like an imposter, and she was unable to see the evidence that God was calling her to preach. But I saw it, and I felt confirmation from the Holy Spirit that I needed to tell her what happened to me when she preached.

Through this conversation with Ashley I heard her pain in the many noes she had heard throughout her life because of her call. I heard about the many times she had wrestled with herself when she got excited about God calling her forward into something new. I could not believe it. I did not realize how blessed I was to grow up in a denomination and church that supported my calling to ministry. In that moment, I realized that many more people in the world were called, but because of their own doubt and the words of others, they were not fulfilling God's call upon their lives.

> Who has encouraged you? Who has spoken words of death to you?

I think it was in that moment I realized that part of my calling in the world for God was helping these people who heard "no" from others but who were clearly called to answer God's calling upon their lives. I was very frank and direct with Ashley as I told her that I thought she was called to ministry and that I wanted to be there the day she got ordained. She laughed, saying that was not going to happen; but God had other plans.

This past year, there I sat, crying proud-mom tears while watching the live stream of Ashley being ordained as an elder in The United Methodist Church (due to COVID, I was unable to travel to Texas). It has been a long road, but along the way Ashley stopped listening to the voices of others who clearly did not recognize her call, and she started listening more closely to the voice of God.

I share this story with you because I do not want anything or anyone to stop you from answering God's calling upon your life. There are a million reasons to say no to God; but in our yeses to God, we find peace, freedom, and a way forward with hope. Today, Ashley serves at a large church and has started a new worship service to reach people in her community. She is a powerful preacher, prophet, and deep lover of God's people. I am so blessed to have Ashley in my life and am so thankful that her call was not silenced.

Like Isaiah, Ashley said yes to God and is continuing to do amazing things. So, friends, do not sell yourselves short because you cannot imagine all the amazing things that God is calling you to do, if only you will say, "Here am I; send me!" (Isa 6:8).

Recognizing our own worth is important in the ministry that God calls us to do. We must be confident in the calling God has placed in our lives. Keeping this confidence and assurance of the calling that God has placed on our lives will help us continue to serve God even when life gets hard. Ministry is not for the faint of heart. Over the years you will experience words of death and limitation prophecies being spoken over you. But if you listen more to God and the body of Christ, and less to the voices that are trying to tear you down, you will find a way to continue to say yes to God.

PRAY

Wrestle with me, God, when I feel unworthy of this calling. Wrestle with me when I feel as though I am experiencing death instead of life. Wrestle with me when I feel that I am an imposter. Wrestle with me when I question my call due to the "limitation prophecies" that have been spoken over my life. Help me to hear you clearly and be able to block out the noise of the culture of constant comparison. Wrestle with me until I am able to say: "Here am I; send me!" Amen.

REFLECT

1. When have you or someone you know felt like an imposter?
2. What are "unclean lips"?
3. Think of some examples of limitation prophecies. What happens to someone who hears negativity over and over? What can a person do to counteract limitation prophecies?
4. What does God need to purify in you? Where do you need forgiveness and reconciliation in your life? In the life of your community?
5. Who has spoken a blessing of life upon you? How did it make you feel? When have you spoken a blessing over someone else? How did that feel?

LISTEN

"You Say" by Lauren Daigle
Go to: https://www.youtube.com/watch?v=sIaT8Jl2zpI.

JOURNAL

How can you tell that God is speaking to you? Pray through Psalm 51:10-12.

3
Wrestling with Call
MARY

In the sixth month the angel Gabriel was sent by God to a town in Galilee called Nazareth, to a virgin engaged to a man whose name was Joseph, of the house of David. The virgin's name was Mary. And he came to her and said, "Greetings, favored one! The Lord is with you." But she was much perplexed by his words and pondered what sort of greeting this might be. The angel said to her, "Do not be afraid, Mary, for you have found favor with God. And now, you will conceive in your womb and bear a son, and you will name him Jesus. He will be great and will be called the Son of the Most High, and the Lord God will give to him the throne of his ancestor David. He will reign over the house of Jacob forever, and of his kingdom there will be no end." Mary said to the angel, "How can this be, since I am a virgin?" The angel said to her, "The Holy Spirit will come upon you, and the power of the Most High will overshadow you; therefore the child to be born will be holy; he will be called Son of God. And now, your relative Elizabeth in her old age has also conceived a son; and this is the sixth month for her who was said to be barren. For nothing will be impossible with God." Then Mary said, "Here am I, the servant of the

Lord; let it be with me according to your word." Then the angel departed from her. (Luke 1:26-38)

SCRIPTURE TELLS US that when Mary first encountered the angel Gabriel, she was afraid. However, Mary was not just afraid of the abruptness in which Gabriel appeared to her. Scholars tell us that Mary would have been familiar with the folkloric story about "a jealous angel who appeared on a bride's wedding night each time she married and killed her bridegroom."[1] When Gabriel appeared, Mary may have thought that he was this dreaded angel who had come to stop her wedding and kill her husband. Only after she realized that Gabriel was an angel of the Lord could she begin to listen to him.

Mary had a lot to lose in answering God's call. She was a poor teenager, and commentary tells us that she was "a peasant woman from the tribe of Judah, and in the line of King David."[2] In that day, Jewish women did not go to the synagogue to learn scripture but were instead taught how to be wives and take care of the home.[3] We see that Mary was following the normal trajectory of her time. She was betrothed to Joseph, which meant that she had already entered into a legally binding contract to marry him and that he had already made a payment, a bride price, to Mary's family upon their engagement.[4] For all legal purposes, Mary and Joseph were married, but they had most likely entered into the yearlong period before they consummated their marriage.

Weighing the Cost

Mary then encountered the angel Gabriel. It must be said that joy was not the first feeling that Mary experienced when she found out that she was going to be the mother of the Messiah. In fact, she may have been in shock. Imagine a teenager hearing this kind of news. Think of the teenagers in your life and how they might handle news like this. How can anyone even process this type of news? I am sure that Mary was fearful to become pregnant with a baby that was not

Joseph's because, in this time, becoming pregnant out of wedlock was, in most cases, punishable by death. She probably had so many thoughts running through her mind about what was going to happen to her. During this time, men got married in their teens if they had the means to support a family, and women could be married as early as twelve.[5] So Mary may have been as young as twelve years old when God called her to this mighty task.

Mary was probably more responsible than most teens, because of her upbringing, but still she had been given a great responsibility, one that could cost her very life. It seems that Mary was still in disbelief, so Gabriel told her that her cousin Elizabeth was also pregnant in her old age, proving to her that "nothing will be impossible with God" (Luke 1:37). What is amazing is that Mary did not miss a beat. Unlike the prophets who came before her, Mary was not only called to use her voice for the Lord, she was also called to use her entire being as an offering to God. What has always struck me the most about her response is that she had no hesitation. Mary immediately opened herself to God's plan for her life. Luke's Gospel tells us that she said, "Here am I, the servant of the Lord; let it be with me according to your word" (v. 38). What an amazing servant of God.

Wrestling with call is another aspect in this spiritual wrestling match of discernment with God. Through baptism we are all called to use our gifts for the Lord, yet God does call some people to very specific tasks. Maybe God has called you to be a missionary, a teacher, or a social worker. Or perhaps God is calling you to work at a local church or in a nonprofit agency. With God's help, and the help of the community of Christ, we are called to further discern how God is calling us to serve.

The next faithful step is to be able to understand what God is calling you to do, even if you don't know the full impact of your response. What do you love to do? What gives life to you and brings you joy? Yes, God may call you beyond the comforts of your everyday life, but God may also be calling you to serve where you are. Be open to how God is speaking to you through the presence and power of the Holy Spirit. This same Holy Spirit will give you affirmation and peace once you have discovered how God is calling you to serve next.

Mary had been called to a very specific task that no one had ever been asked to do before, which makes her call story one of the most powerful call stories in the Bible. But she did not know—how could she?—where God would lead her. Mary was a teenage girl in whom God chose to do a mighty work: carry, bear, and raise the Christ child.

One of the things I love the most about Mary's call story is her directness. Mary did not beat around the bush. Once Gabriel told her that she would bear the Christ child, she simply asked, "How can this be?" (v. 34). While Mary probably asked this question as a matter of practicality, you may find yourself asking God the same question. How can it be that God has called you to serve at this moment in time?

We see that Mary models for us that it is okay to ask God questions. It is okay to wrestle with our call, especially when we may not fully understand what God is calling us to do. It is okay to seek affirmation from the community of faith, and it is okay to take a trip and talk to a trusted friend or family member. You may be wary of answering God's call at this moment in history because this is not an easy moment in the life of the world. But it never is.

Christianity is no longer the priority of many people, and church has been replaced by sports, travel teams, TV, work, and so much more. Many people who have grown up going to church have now turned away from organized religion. Instead of lamenting the state of the world, we are called to see it as an opportunity. What gifts can you bring to build up the kingdom of God? How can you help the church be creative about being the church in the community at this moment in time? The church's landscape is changing, and this brings many exciting possibilities for worship and creative faith expressions outside the church walls. We, like Mary, are called to ask the same question she asked: "How can it be that God would invite me to partner in ministry?" This question is less about doubt in ourselves and more of an exclamation about our awe-inspiring God. So, like Mary, how can we respond, "Let it be with me according to your word"?

Confronting Fear

As we wrestle with our call, we must confront our fear. Many times in our lives, fear stops us from responding to God's call. We fear the uncertainty of our future. Where will God call us to serve? Will we be able to make enough money to live and support a family? Are we capable of the task ahead? We fear whether we will be able to continue the ministry to which we have been called. We fear what others will think of us.

> What are you afraid of? What are you afraid of giving up?

Just as Mary knew that answering God's call would require sacrifice, the truth is that ministry is hard. There are some very difficult days, but you also experience a depth of humanity and life that you would never experience otherwise. You also see people accept Jesus Christ and find peace. You are present with people through some of the most difficult moments of their lives and celebrate with people in the best moments of their lives. Through its many highs and lows, the life of ministry is a full one. Through a life of ministry, you get to experience the face of God through the many faces of the people you pastor. The life of ministry is a life of hope. Mary teaches us that God's call is to move beyond fear.

I wonder what fears you may have on your heart today. Maybe it is leaving a job you have had a long time. Maybe it is fear of the unknown and wondering how God will provide a way forward for you. If we are honest, we all must admit that we do have some fear in answering God's call. We should not be afraid of this fear. Instead, I like to think of this fear as reverent. We fear God, not just because we fear the unknown but because we serve an amazing and almighty

God. Through our scripture from Luke, Mary shows us how to move beyond fear.

We can move beyond fear when we recognize that ministry does require sacrifice. In the moment that Mary said yes to God, she probably could not have imagined the sacrifice she would endure, the hardest of which would be watching her son be crucified. The Gospel of John tells us that Mary was indeed at the foot of the cross watching her son Jesus die (19:25-27). In his book *Final Words from the Cross*, Adam Hamilton shares the many sacrifices that Mary experienced:

> It was Mary who, when called to risk her life and give up all of her dreams in order to carry, deliver, and raise the Messiah, replied, "Here I am, the servant of the Lord." . . . It was Mary who carried the Son of God in her womb, having supplied the human material needed for the Incarnation. . . . This woman who stood by the cross seeking desperately to console and give hope to her dying son paid a great price for our salvation.[6]

I often wonder if we were to ask Mary, would she do it all again? I think her answer would still be a resounding yes! None of us know what God has in store for us when we say yes to God, but we must say yes even when we encounter opposition from others.

We Move Forward in Call Together

For a long time, it bothered me that some people did not celebrate God's call upon my life and some just thought it was odd. When I graduated from Virginia Tech and prepared to go to Duke Divinity School, many of my classmates asked me, "Why would you do that?" Some thought it was a phase. Although, by the grace of God, I did have many family, friends, and mentors who celebrated with me.

Having a solid support system is vital to answering God's call. Mary was blessed to have the support of her cousin Elizabeth. Once Mary encountered the angel Gabriel and heard the life changing news that she was to be the mother of the Son of God, she left her home and traveled to see Elizabeth. I believe she also went on this journey to receive further affirmation about what the angel had told her. Was it true that Elizabeth was pregnant in her old age? In Mary's encounter with Elizabeth, Mary not only received affirmation of the angel's words, she also received a blessing from Elizabeth. After receiving this blessing, Mary was able to celebrate God's call upon her life more fully.

The scripture from Luke 1:46-56 is known to many as "Mary's Magnificat" due to the very first line when Mary says, "My soul magnifies the Lord" (v. 46). This was Mary's song of praise to God for being chosen to be the mother of Jesus Christ. So often on Christmas Eve we sing the song: "Mary, Did You Know?" This is a beautiful song that talks about Mary bearing Jesus Christ and the things he would grow up to do, ultimately saving us from our sins. If you read the Magnificat, it seems that although there is no way that Mary could in that moment fully realize who Jesus would be, she certainly understood what he had been called to do.

Mary did know who Jesus was. When God chose her to bear the Christ, she embodied the words she spoke. In Luke 1:52 she says, "He has brought down the powerful from their thrones, / and lifted up the lowly." Mary was poor and humble—from the lower rungs of society—yet she was chosen; she was important. She was imperfect, yet she was blessed. She was a servant who aided in God's fulfillment of prophecy. Mary understood that Jesus was bringing redemption to the people.

Social status would be turned upside down, and the lowly would be exalted. We see this upside-down hierarchy later in Jesus's life through his healing ministry. Jesus healed many people with leprosy, who were no longer allowed to live in the community. Through God's healing, they were brought back into the community and into relationship with their family and friends. Ultimately, they were able to experience redemption. Through saying yes to God, Mary took part in Christ's ministry of redemption of the world.

CHAPTER 3

We are called to participate in Christ's ministry of redemption as well. In the moment of Mary's call, she was changed and blessed. Her identity changed from wife of Joseph and poor teenager to mother of Christ. She was blessed because she got to partake in God's ministry in the world. We, too, will find joy and blessing from answering God's call.

We also need others to celebrate God's call in our lives and our newfound identities in Christ. Whether your support system is made up of your biological family or your chosen family, you will need people who will continue to affirm your gifts and support you on this journey of discernment. If you do not yet have a strong support system, work on cultivating relationships with those around you who bring life to you and speak encouragement to your soul. Look for a mentor or spend time with a close friend who "gets" you. That way, when fears crop up, you can check those fears against people who know you and who see your gifts for mission and ministry.

> What are some ways that God calls people today?

Listening for God

For some, God's call is obvious. Moses saw a burning bush, Jonah was swallowed by a large fish, Samuel was called by name, and Mary was called by the angel Gabriel. Some people are blessed by an amazing community of faith that affirms their call and encourages them to move forward in their discernment process. For some people, God's call is so obvious that they may feel they have no choice but to answer God.

For others, God's call may be more subtle and mysterious. For instance, Elisha could have missed his calling from God if he hadn't been paying close attention. First Kings 19 recounts the moment Elisha is called to do the work of the Lord (vv. 16-21). This is an interesting call story to say the least. Elisha is in the field minding his own business. He is taking care of his oxen when all of the sudden the prophet Elijah shows up, throws him a mantle—his outer garment—and keeps going. Yet, somehow, Elisha understands the significance of this moment. In fact, scholars tell us Elisha's response to his call. He "sacrifices . . . the tools of his trade, slaughtering the oxen, and using the equipment that comes with them for fuel."[7] For Elisha, there would be no going back. He had been chosen by God to complete Elijah's work (v. 16). Elisha sacrificed the comfort of his home and profession to do the work of God.

Like Elisha, some may experience God's call through another person's action, so we always must be on the lookout for how God is calling us to serve. One thing is certain: throughout the Bible God called many different people to do God's important work. Although some call stories have similarities, it is important to remember that each call story is unique to God and the individual being called. Psalm 139 reminds us that God knows us better than we know ourselves; so when we are called, we must trust and believe that we have been called for a reason.

I believe the most difficult thing you will experience on this journey is responding to God's call. God is always calling us, but are we always listening? As we go through our daily to-do list, so often God gets pushed to the bottom of the list. We may say, "I'll get to that later, God" or "One day, when I have more time to pursue my calling." Life is fragile, and the best time to answer God's call is right now! You can make a million excuses, but once you say yes to God then you, too, can move forward in God's plan for your life. Answering God's call is never easy; but I promise you it is worth it, and it will also benefit the lives of so many other people.

> Are you ready to say yes to God?

Perhaps you have discerned that God is calling you to mission or ministry but are unable to take the next steps. I think a lot of people

CHAPTER 3

get stuck in this part of the journey because they realize that once they move forward their lives may change forever. Spoiler alert: once you say yes to God's call, your life *will* change forever. I believe it will change for the better.

I take comfort in the many stories in the Bible of people who needed a minute before they were ready to respond to God's call. I have always loved the story of Jonah. Jonah knew what it was like to be called by God and not be ready to respond. In fact, Jonah tried to run away from God, which we all know is impossible, but he thought it was worth a try. My favorite part of this scripture is that God did not give up on Jonah. Jonah 3:1 says, "The word of the Lord came to Jonah a second time." God called Jonah a second time because God knew he was capable; God knew that he could help the Ninevites. God did not give up on Jonah, even when Jonah was ready to give up on God.

Through Jonah's second call we are reminded that God will continue to pursue us and God will continue to call us. So, even though we may run, even though we may hide, even though we may not be ready to serve, God will continue to invite us anyway. Jonah went through many trials before he finally answered God's call. He almost drowned, he was swallowed by a big fish, and during that period he probably wondered if he would survive. Yet God preserved Jonah's life and sent him forward with a purpose. So, today, please do not feel guilty if you have not yet been able to answer God's call. Do not worry; God will keep calling you. It may be through reading Scripture or through prayer; it may be as you minister to God's people or when you are out in God's beautiful creation. God may call you through the words of a pastor, friend, family member, or stranger. Or God may even call you through a movie scene. The important thing is that you are open to what God is calling you to do next.

In my current ministry setting, I have been given the joy of watching God's calling upon the life of one of my parishioners. On my very first Sunday I preached a sermon about God's calling upon my life, and as I looked out at the congregation, I saw Jeff leaning forward in his seat actively engaged in the words I was sharing. I continued to notice that God was pointing things out to me about Jeff and his gifts for ministry. Jeff had a passion for Scripture. He had experienced a kind of reawakening to his faith after the death of his father, and his joy for the Bible was contagious. I asked him to co-lead and lead various Bible studies, which I could tell he thoroughly enjoyed. Eventually I asked Jeff to preach on Laity Sunday, and he delivered a powerful message about God's grace. Jeff also had a heart for God's people and was able to naturally build relationships with those in the church. It was so obvious to me that God was calling Jeff to the ministry, so one evening before Bible study I shared this with Jeff.

To my surprise, Jeff knew God was calling him but felt unable to answer God's calling at the moment. Jeff needed this affirmation to take a step forward. Since that time, Jeff has started attending seminary; and this past June, I watched the livestream and saw the moment that Jeff became a licensed local pastor in the Virginia Conference UMC. As I was called to a new appointment, Jeff became the pastor of the church that had nurtured his call and benefitted from his leadership and spirituality.

In experiencing Jeff's call to ministry, God has reminded me that answering God's call is a process. It is not something we do in one moment; it is something we do each and every day with our lives. Each day, we take one step closer to doing all the things God would have us do. I give thanks to God that I have been able to witness God calling Jeff, and through this call I have seen him changed and blessed.

Wrestling with Call Spotlight: Rev. Pat Watkins

There I found myself, snorkeling in the Chesapeake Bay looking for sea grass. This was not how I envisioned myself being in mission, but I was there because Pat Watkins invited me. In my young adult years

CHAPTER 3

I had some amazing mentors to look up to, and Pat was one of them. Pat was soft-spoken, but when he did speak up everyone listened to his words of wisdom and care.

At a young age Pat felt called by God, but he did not see himself working within the confines of the local church. He wrestled with God over where God was calling him to serve. His first missionary trip was to Nigeria, where he learned how to live off the seasons of the land. This type of life really resonated with Pat as he saw that we are created to need the earth and vice versa. Something clicked for Pat while he was at this missionary appointment, and he wanted to continue to learn more about how we can live out our faith by taking care of God's creation. Pat went back to school and learned as much as he could about environmental science.

Pat wanted to move forward in this newfound passion for ministry and mission, but he was uncertain if there was a place like this for him in ministry. So he started sharing his passion for caring for God's creation where he was. Soon, others started to get excited about serving God in this way. Due to Pat's passion and determination, more and more people became excited about living out their faith through caring for God's creation. When there did not seem to be a place for Pat to serve, God made a way. Pat's call was not actualized in one moment. He spent many years leading up to the moment where others recognized and validated his call, but he never gave up because he knew this was the work that God had called him to do. Before his retirement, Pat was serving at a global level as the first missionary to be appointed to care for God's creation.

Pat's continued advice to those who are discerning is that God can use your gifts and passion for ministry. Do not become discouraged if you feel that your call does not fit within the institutionalized church. If you know that God has called you, don't give up. Celebrate the gifts you have and use them to serve God!

Maybe you have been discouraged and, like Jonah, have run away from God because you could not see a place where you could serve. Or perhaps God is calling you into ministry or to be a missionary after you have had a professional career. Maybe God is calling you to a different kind of ministry, one that you never envisioned. None of us are ever truly ready or fully equipped to do the work of God, but God gives us strength and helps us.

My hope for you is that you can give voice to a calling that God has placed upon your life. That call may be to teach Sunday school or lead the youth group or to be a pastor. That calling may be to serve as a missionary. Whatever it is, my prayer is that you would move forward in answering God's call. The first step is to tell someone you trust—someone who will be excited for you. Then tell your pastor, who will further help you discern where God is calling you to go. My prayer is that you continue this ministry of call by acknowledging and celebrating God's call in others. You can be a sounding board for others as they discern their call. You can pray for them. You can help them give voice to their calling and help to bless them on their journey of discernment.

> How can you support others in their call? How do you want to be supported?

In answering God's call, our lives will be forever changed like Mary's, but the blessing we experience will lie in seeing Christ at work in the world each day. May God continue to give us the strength to surrender our lives to God!

PRAY

Wrestle with me, God, when I have more excuses than reasons to say yes to you. Wrestle with me when I am not ready to voice my call to my friends and family. Wrestle with me when I am afraid of the uncertainty that comes from surrender. Wrestle with me as I realize the gravity of the life of sacrifice and responsibility to which I have been called. Wrestle with me until I, too, can say, "Let it be with me according to your word." Amen.

CHAPTER 3

REFLECT

1. What is your favorite excuse? What excuses do you make to God when you are not ready to do something God has asked you to do?
2. Who is someone in the Bible that you admire? Who is someone in the Bible with whom you identify? What is their relationship with God? How does that match up with your story?
3. What/Who do you need to surrender to God?
4. How can you listen better to God? How might God be calling you to serve?
5. What do you feel passionate about? Might that be a way that God is calling you?

LISTEN

"Come to the Altar" by Elevation Worship
https://www.youtube.com/watch?v=rYQ5yXCc_CA

JOURNAL

How is God calling you to serve today?

4
Wrestling with Identity
PAUL

Meanwhile Saul, still breathing threats and murder against the disciples of the Lord, went to the high priest and asked him for letters to the synagogues at Damascus, so that if he found any who belonged to the Way, men or women, he might bring them bound to Jerusalem. Now as he was going along and approaching Damascus, suddenly a light from heaven flashed around him. He fell to the ground and heard a voice saying to him, "Saul, Saul, why do you persecute me?" He asked, "Who are you, Lord?" The reply came, "I am Jesus, whom you are persecuting. But get up and enter the city, and you will be told what you are to do." The men who were traveling with him stood speechless because they heard the voice but saw no one. Saul got up from the ground, and though his eyes were open, he could see nothing; so they led him by the hand and brought him into Damascus. For three days he was without sight, and neither ate nor drank. (Acts 9:1-9)

A BURST OF BRIGHT light was Saul's first clue that Jesus had come into his life. Then he found he could not see anything at all.

CHAPTER 4

Have you ever been in a dark room and suddenly someone turned on a bright light? An encounter like this can be a shock to the senses. We can feel as if we are not ready to experience God in this way, yet just as in our faith, Christ calls us out of the darkness and into the "marvelous light" (1 Pet 2:9). Sometimes we cannot see the light of Christ until we find ourselves in darkness.

Right after Saul saw the burst of light, he immediately found himself in darkness. Until that moment, in his own mind Saul thought he was doing what God wanted him to do. Saul was a devout Jew. At his core, his identity was dependent upon his keeping to the letter of the law. And he felt called to maintain the purity of the Jewish faith by all means necessary. That meant stamping out dissident voices, such as those raised by followers of the Way—as followers of Jesus were called before they were called Christians. But Saul let power go to his head, and he became more interested in persecuting Christians and less interested in sharing God's Word.

Many scholars believe that Saul was able to gain this type of power because "he belonged to a *politeuma*, a Jewish community given the right to govern itself through Jewish law, tradition, and institutions."[1] So Saul, unchecked by his own community, started focusing on stopping all Christians from practicing their faith. Scripture tells us that Saul stood nearby as the disciple Stephen was stoned (Acts 7:58). At the beginning of Acts 9 we see that Saul was still on this mission. In fact, he was on his way to the synagogues in Damascus, under the authority of the high priest in Jerusalem, to root out more Christians.

Not until his powerful encounter with the risen Christ did Saul believe that Jesus was the Son of God—the fulfillment of the law that Saul was sworn to uphold—and he realized that his so-called ministry up until that moment in time was costing people their lives. Being struck by blinding light gave Saul three days in his own darkness to wrestle with who he really was and what, up until that point, he had given his life to do.

During this time, the Bible tells us Saul was praying (Acts 9:11). I always wonder what words he uttered to God. Did he say, "Help me!" or "I'm sorry, God"? Did he say, "Thank you for saving me," or "I'm grateful that you revealed yourself to me," or perhaps a combination? But for all this, God did not leave him but brought him in touch with the body of Christ.

> How have you encountered Christ? Do you know people who have had a "Damascus Road" experience?

The beautiful thing about answering God's call is that we do not do it by ourselves. The first lesson that God taught Saul was that he needed to rely on the body of Christ. The beauty of Saul's call story is that it involves a follower of Christ—one of those Saul was out to get—a man named Ananias. God spoke to Ananias in a vision and told him to go and give Saul sight. I would imagine that Ananias was not excited about this assignment. He basically said, "Are you sure, God? This man has great authority and is persecuting your people. Are you sure I should go and help him?" But as a good servant of the Lord, he said, "Here I am" (v. 10).

Just as the community of faith helped to unbind Lazarus from the literal trappings of death, in this scripture we see that God used Ananias to help free Saul from the trappings of his sin against God's people.

> So Ananias went and entered the house. He laid his hands on Saul and said: "Brother Saul, the Lord Jesus, who appeared to you on your way here, has sent me so that you may regain your sight and be filled with the Holy Spirit." And immediately something like scales fell from his eyes, and his sight was restored. Then he got up and was baptized, and after taking some food, he regained his strength.
>
> For several days he was with the disciples in Damascus, and immediately he began to proclaim Jesus in the synagogues, saying: "He is the Son of God." (Acts 9:17-20)

CHAPTER 4

From darkness to light, from blindness to sight—in this moment of transformation, we are shown the path of discipleship. We encounter Christ; we are nurtured by Christ's body; we are baptized and enter into a covenant with God and the community of faith; we share in the sacrament of Communion; we spend time in study and worship; and then we are sent out to share the good news of Christ with others by the power of the Holy Spirit.

As we know, Saul became known as Paul (the Greek, *Paulos*, and the Latin, *Paulus*, are transliterations of the Hebrew, *Saul*)—a powerful evangelist. He could relate with Jews because he could say, "I used to be one of you; I used to not believe that Jesus was the Son of God, but then Jesus confronted me and gave me new sight and the power of the Holy Spirit!" He could also relate to Greeks and Romans because he probably spoke Greek and was a Roman citizen. Paul had the gifts and graces to accomplish God's mission even before he met Christ on the road. Paul was a powerful evangelist because he took the gifts he already had and combined them with the passion he now had for Jesus Christ.

Through the years as I have journeyed with many people who were discerning God's call, I have realized that there is a common misconception that you have to give up all of who you are to be a servant of the Lord. Does serving God require sacrifice and surrender? Yes. Does serving God mean that God will continue to change you by the power of the Holy Spirit? Yes. But you are called to use the gifts you already have, all for the glory of God.

As a pastor it is beautiful to watch these "aha moments" happen in my congregation. "Aha moments" happen when people realize they are already in ministry and mission where they are. They happen when people realize they can use their gifts of architecture, finance, music, social work, and education all for the glory of God. These aha moments happen when others recognize God's gifts within us and share with us what they see. I have been blessed to have so many people support me in this way.

When I was nineteen years old and had just completed my first year of college, I was looking for a summer job. In the meantime I started going back to my home church. It was so comforting to be back in my spiritual home. My pastor asked me what I would be doing that summer. I responded that I was looking for a job. I did not realize it in that moment, but the trajectory of my summer had already begun with that one conversation. You see, my pastor, Rhonda, had the gift of noticing. She noticed that I was struggling with my pastoral identity, and she took time out of her busy schedule to ask me about it. After one of these conversations she asked me, "Do you think you would like to come and be our ministry intern this summer?"

> What jobs have you had? How did you get them? What did you learn?

I was surprised, as I never thought this internship was a possibility for my summer. That week, Rhonda had many conversations with key leaders in the church; and they decided to offer me the internship, the first of its kind at my home church. I was elated; I did not realize that both God and Rhonda had plans for me. Throughout the summer I was given so many opportunities to try all the different facets of ministry. I answered phones in the church office, sat in on various meetings, and went on pastoral care visits. My last assignment was to preach my first sermon.

> When you look in a mirror, what three words describe what you see?

One of my first assignments from Rhonda was to read a book and do a book presentation to the church leadership. After that, I found out that reading this book with your pastor was the first step in the candidacy process for ministry. It just so happened that I was already moving forward in the process to become a pastor before I even realized it. Rhonda saw

CHAPTER 4

something in me, something I did not see in myself. She saw that God was calling me to ministry and that I did not know how to respond. She saw that I could use my gifts for and love of music all for the glory of God. By giving me this internship, Rhonda helped me discern further the direction to go to answer God's call upon my life. I will forever be grateful to her for that summer of discernment as I grew in my understanding of my pastoral identity.

Where Do I Fit?

As we answer God's call, we wrestle with our identity: Who are we, and who is God calling us to be? Where do we fit in God's mission? While we may be more or less aware of our gifts and our weaknesses, the core of who we are is much deeper than our personality or self-assessment. Throughout our lives we develop our identity, the person we think we are. We go through hills and valleys, and these experiences shape how we see ourselves. God can see through any façade we may try to erect. God knows our identity because it centers on Jesus Christ. I have always loved Philippians 4:13: "I can do all things through [Christ] who strengthens me." God continues to teach us through Scripture that to do the holy work of ministry and mission we must recognize that our identity starts and ends with God's love for us.

> What are you good at? What are you passionate about?

You may find yourself in this discovery process. You may be wrestling with God over who God is calling you to be. You, like Saul (later renamed "Paul"), may have had a Damascus Road experience and feel that God is confronting you. Or perhaps your experience of God's call has been more subtle. No matter how you have experienced God calling you to serve, one thing is certain: the light of Christ will continue to lead you forward in this period of discernment.

From Darkness to Light

One story that does not get a lot of mention in the Bible is when Paul and Silas were in prison and there was a great earthquake (Acts 16:16-40). After the earthquake the prison doors opened wide, and all the prisoners had a way to escape. This was wonderful news, unless you were the jailer, the authority in charge. The jailer realized there was no way he could stop the escape of all the prisoners and decided that the only thing he could do was take his own life because, in those days, an escaped prisoner meant death to those who held the keys. Paul realized what was happening and told all the prisoners to stay put. Even more amazing is that his fellow prisoners listened. That evening Paul went to the home of the jailer where he was welcomed for dinner, and there the jailer and his whole family gave their lives to Jesus Christ. That night, Paul offered Christ and an entire household was saved. That night could have ended in darkness for so many people, but because of Paul's care for the jailer, everyone got to live to see the light of another day.

Today you may find yourself in the darkness of confusion. You may have already been called by God, but now what? You may be grieving the loss of everything familiar as you go into the great unknown. You may have encountered pushback from family or friends who dampened some excitement you had at first. Or maybe the darkness you are experiencing is doubt. You may be thinking, "God, I can't start over. Not now." Whatever darkness you may be experiencing, know that God will meet you in that place and lead you out, and the body of Christ will be there by your side.

The Power of Seeing and Being Seen

Interestingly, a new narrative is being told in pop culture. For so long a good leader was considered to be someone who was a workaholic, someone who would sacrifice themselves for the good of the company and who modeled extreme effectiveness. This model is changing.

CHAPTER 4

Research is showing that people are more responsive to a leader who is vulnerable rather than a leader who is strong all the time.

In her Ted Talk entitled "The Power of Vulnerability," Brene Brown, a research professor at the University of Houston Graduate College of Social Work, speaks to this idea. She says, "In order for connection to happen we have to allow ourselves to be seen, really seen."[2] In order for us to connect to other people, we must be vulnerable. This is the place where we find Saul, completely vulnerable. He was blind and had to rely on a stranger, Ananias, to help him. Yet in his vulnerability, this surrender to the call of Jesus Christ, Saul gained new life and a new identity.

Paul has a powerful story because we can relate to it. In his quest to persecute others, he was consumed by his cause. We all know how it feels to be consumed by something, whether it is a project or assignment or worry, shame, anger, unforgiveness, or pride. We know how it feels to be blinded to the love and grace of God, even when God is right beside us.

> When was a time you were consumed by something or fixated on someone?

Scripture makes no mistake in telling us that Paul was blind for three days before he regained his sight. This was the same pattern for Jesus's resurrection. Just as the disciples waited three days until the light of the world shone again, Saul waited three days to experience a moment of resurrection in his life, a time to die to his sins and be risen with Christ. Paul went forward from that moment a changed person and became one of the most effective evangelists of his time.

Paul had to be confronted by Christ before he was ready to spend time in discernment and to change into the person God was calling him to be. Just as God confronted Paul on the road to Damascus, God still wrestles with us so that we, too, will follow the invitation of the risen Christ. Sometimes we find ourselves unable to heed Jesus's call in the moment. But remember, God gave Saul three days to figure it out; and I believe that God will lead you in your time of discernment about where God is calling you to go next.

The most impactful thing about Paul's call story is that in his mind he thought he saw what God wanted him to do. He was gaining power and prestige. He wanted to be a leader, and he thought he was becoming the leader he always hoped he would be. After this pivotal moment, Paul's life was not about power. It was about surrendering humbly to the call of Christ—seeing himself as God saw him. From this moment on, Paul found himself on a completely different trajectory with a completely different identity. Yet he adapted. He took the gifts he had had before, and he applied them to his call. This is what made him so influential; he was just as comfortable talking to political rulers as he was sailors. Paul did not have to start over completely after his Damascus Road experience. He already had a lot to work with, but the new thing he had to do was trust in where God was leading him.

You may find yourself reading this chapter after you have had a great career. You may be wondering, "How can I leave everything so familiar?" You may think it is too late in life to answer God's call. I am here to tell you, friend, it is never too late to answer God's call on your life. We all have questions when God calls. All we can do is trust in God and rely on the body of Christ to support us. God will lead you forward; and, like Paul, you should get ready because you are about to have some adventures!

The good news is that, like Paul, you can use the gifts you already have to serve God. Although Paul's life changed drastically that day on the road to Damascus, he continued to use the skills he had gained throughout his life, but now he used them to share the good news of Jesus Christ. You may be gifted in mechanical engineering, music, or technology. You can use these gifts as you equip disciples. Surrendering to God's call does not mean that you give up who you are; it means that you take who God has created you to be and serve where you are. It also means that you are willing to go to new places beyond your wildest imagination.

CHAPTER 4

The Adventure of Discipleship

God took Paul all over the Roman world. Today we take travel for granted and can get to even faraway places in several days. But in Paul's day travel was difficult and even life threatening. Also, even though Paul was self-employed as a tentmaker, he still had to rely on others to provide for his needs. He risked his life in each voyage that he made and in each town he traveled. He even got into a shipwreck (Acts 27). But through it all Paul never forgot who he was. He was called by God to share the good news of Christ with Jews and Greeks alike so that we could all be one in the body of Christ (1 Cor 12:12).

Paul's impact of evangelism and encouragement live on through the words he left us, words that encourage us to practice our faith: "If God is for us who is against us?" (Rom 8:31); "[Love] ... endures all things" (1 Cor 13:7); "Give thanks in all circumstances" (1 Thess 5:18). And you may have your own favorite of Paul's scriptures to add.

Authentic Living as Who You Are

Not only does Paul's eloquence with words live on, so does his model of living out his faith daily. Paul showed his change in identity when he started going by his Roman name, Paul. Unlike Jacob, who was given a new name by God, Scripture shows us that Paul chose to go by this name, because that is how he signed his letters. By using his Roman name of Paul instead of his Hebrew name of Saul, he would be able to reach more people as he traveled to preach the good news.[3]

> How did you get your name?

God speaks to us by calling us by name to do the work of the Lord. Jesus's words to Saul started with calling his name. In the garden of Eden, God called out Adam's name as God came to find him. God continues to call us by name as well. Today God may be calling you to do something completely different from anything you have ever done before. Maybe God is calling you to ministry or mission, or maybe God is calling you to get more involved in your church. Perhaps God is calling you from the corporate world to the nonprofit sector. However God calls you, whether it is subtle or confrontational, I pray you answer the call. My hope is that you will also find a new identity in Christ as you continue to pursue your call.

Sharing Your Story

Paul reminds us that it is important to tell our stories and use all of who we are for God's glory. I hope you get the chance to tell your story to your pastor or a trusted friend. Share how God is moving in your life, and you may hear some amazing stories in return. Just as Ananias was a key part of Saul's conversion story, God gives us the community of faith to affirm God's call.

If you are feeling God's call to ministry and mission, the next step is to have your call affirmed by your faith community. This means that your church sees the same gifts in you that God sees so that you can move forward in this holy work. My youth director Fran was the first person to voice my call to ministry. Before it was even a thought in my mind, Fran kept pointing me in the direction of serving others, which I happened to love. She made it possible for me to attend thirteen mission trips by the time I graduated from high school. She helped me to secure funds and make the plans so that I could attend events such as helping to rebuild a church that had been burned down by the Ku Klux Klan; events such as Harvest of Hope (founded by Rhonda), where God called me again in the cornfield; and events such as Voices of Youth, where I traveled to Mexico and heard an entire annual conference praying to God at the same time. Fran made it possible for me to have these experiences because she knew that it would help me further discern my call.

When I finally was able to express my call to ministry to Fran, she gave me a knowing smile and said, "I know. I'm glad you finally figured it out!" Fran has been there for me each step of the way. Through the years I have called her when big things have happened to me, telling her it is her fault because she ignited in me a passion for mission and ministry. Fran even came to my ordination service (which is a long service) and took a picture with me after the service in which she is beaming and looking up at me. It is because of Fran, Rhonda, and the countless other members in the body of Christ who recognized my call that I am where I am today. These people gave me the courage to move forward in my call and to claim my identity as pastor.

In The United Methodist Church, this moment of accepting the identity and role of pastor happens at the service of ordination. The bishop lays hands on each individual being ordained and says, "Take authority as an elder [or a deacon] . . . in the name of the Father, and of the Son, and of the Holy Spirit."[4] In this moment the individual person's identity ceases. Their life is no longer their own but belongs to God and the church. The mark of this change in identity is the stole that is laid upon each pastor's shoulders. This stole helps others to recognize pastors and helps them remember that they are yoked in their ministry with Jesus Christ. These symbols of our faith only mean something when we worship in community. No one can answer their call without God's help or the support of the body of Christ. This week, take some time to ask a close friend what gifts they may see in you. Their answers may help you further discern your call and where to go next.

Wrestling with Identity Spotlight: Rev. Dottie Yunger

One of the most unique call stories I have heard is that of Rev. Dottie Yunger. When Dottie was six years old, she experienced a call not to mission or ministry but to marine biology. Her parents took her to the Smithsonian National Museum of Natural History in Washington DC. That day at an ocean exhibit Dottie saw a giant blue whale. This was the moment when she felt called to become a marine biologist. After she completed her degree, she came back to work in that same museum, and her office was under that giant blue whale.

Faith was always important to Dottie, and each Sunday she found herself in her local church. One Sunday she felt God calling her to go to seminary. As she wrestled with this new calling from God, she decided not to tell anyone about what happened. She thought, "Why would a scientist go to seminary? Science and faith don't mix." As she worked up the courage to tell her husband, he replied, "I was wondering if you'd go."

The affirmation of her call did not stop there. She was assigned a wonderful mentor who helped her cultivate her call. This mentor happened to be a UMC pastor as well as a scientist. This was a sign from God, like a bright, flashing light. Then there was another sign. As Dottie was not yet ready to commit to seminary, she decided to try one class on science and religion. Her professor happened to be a retired astrophysicist, and through this one class Dottie had her aha moment and saw that her passion for science and Jesus Christ was a blessing and an avenue for her to serve in ministry. She enrolled in seminary and completed her master of divinity degree and master of theology degree in eco-theology.

Throughout her ministry, Dottie has used her passions for Christ and science to serve God's people. One project she and her church undertook was to bring fresh fish and produce to communities living in food deserts along the Anacostia River. Dottie knew the fish in the river were not safe to eat, but sometimes people had no other option. So she worked with a congregation member who was a scientist and professor and had built a three-acre urban farm for a community a mile from the river. Through this congregation member's partnership with Dottie, this place became the home to the pilot program where fishermen could bring the unsafe fish they caught and trade them for healthy fish. Dottie's passions for faith and science connected her with that community and celebrated the gifts of the body of Christ.

CHAPTER 4

Currently Dottie serves a small United Methodist Church part-time and as a marine biologist at Calvert Marine Museum. She is appointed to both these places as a pastor. This is possible through a program by the General Board of Global Ministries in The United Methodist Church called Earth Keepers. This program trains and equips people who have a passion for the environment to connect this passion with sharing the good news of Jesus Christ. Because Dottie had been through this training, she was able to be appointed in this unique way to pastor people and God's aquatic creation within her own conference. Many of her congregation members volunteer at the museum, and Dottie reminds them that they are in mission and ministry for Jesus Christ as they interact with many different people in the community. Dottie continues to combine her passion for science and her passion for Jesus Christ as she makes disciples. Like the apostle Paul, she uses the gifts she already had and combines them with her passion for Christ as she serves in ministry with God's people.

> What are you passionate about? How can you combine this passion and your passion for Christ?

Like the apostle Paul, you are called to use all of who you are for God's glory. Don't be afraid to share your gifts, even if you feel they don't fit in the life of the church. You will be surprised at what God can do with the things you are passionate about. Sharing our gifts brings the light of Christ to others. May we not be afraid to die to ourselves and rise with Christ so that we can pursue God's call upon our lives and so that God can help us claim our new identity in Christ.

PRAY

Wrestle with me, God, when I cannot see myself in the reflection of the cross. Wrestle with me when I forget who I am and who you have called me to be. Wrestle with me when I am not rooted in your Word and I turn a blind eye to your will. Wrestle with me when I get weighed down by the cost of discipleship and am unable to see the promise of new life. Change my heart, and give me a new identity and purpose to serve you. Amen.

REFLECT

1. Have you or someone you know had a "Damascus Road" experience? What happened?
2. Is there one part of your story that you would like to share?
3. What is the most influential testimony you have ever heard? What made it so powerful?
4. Describe one of your "aha moments."
5. Why is the affirmation of the community of faith so important when answering God's call? How can the church encourage you?

LISTEN

"Who Am I" by Casting Crowns
https://www.youtube.com/watch?v=C53GgUJ6y-Y

JOURNAL

Write down how you believe that God is calling you. How is your call similar to and/or different from that of Paul?

5
Wrestling with Others
DEBORAH

At that time Deborah, a prophetess, wife of Lappidoth, was judging Israel. She used to sit under the palm of Deborah between Ramah and Bethel in the hill country of Ephraim; and the Israelites came up to her for judgment. She sent and summoned Barak son of Abinoam from Kedesh in Naphtali, and said to him, "The LORD, the God of Israel, commands you, 'Go, take position at Mount Tabor, bringing ten thousand from the tribe of Naphtali and the tribe of Zebulun. I will draw out Sisera, the general of Jabin's army, to meet you by the Wadi Kishon with his chariots and his troops; and I will give him into your hand.'" Barak said to her, "If you will go with me, I will go; but if you will not go with me, I will not go." And she said, "I will surely go with you; nevertheless, the road on which you are going will not lead to your glory, for the LORD will sell Sisera into the hand of a woman." Then Deborah got up and went with Barak to Kedesh. Barak summoned Zebulun and Naphtali to Kedesh; and ten thousand warriors went up behind him; and Deborah went up with him. (Judg 4:4-10)

CHAPTER 5

GOD CALLED DEBORAH to be a prophet and a judge, a very unusual position for a woman in her time. She could never have dreamed that God would choose her for this task. Yet she found herself under the palm trees judging cases day in and day out for the Israelites. She used the word of God to speak into people's lives and deliver justice. Deborah was the wife of Lappidoth, which in Hebrew is translated, "the woman of torches."[1] So Deborah's name was "Torch Woman," and she led the way for the Israelite people.

Deborah was named judge after the previous judge, Ehud, died. God chose someone with fire in their belly—someone who could deliver the truth in love—someone who could teach people how to take responsibility for their actions and repent. Deborah was quite successful at her job. Then God called her to do something unexpected: to go from the comforts of the courtroom, or sitting under the palms surrounded by people eager to hear her words, to wrestle to the death with an enemy.

> Think about a time you were asked to do something you had never done before? How did it turn out?

I often wonder if Deborah ever thought she would end up going to war. Many times in ministry, we have one idea of how things will go, and then God steps in and calls us completely out of our comfort zones. Yet nowhere in Scripture do we see Deborah shy away from where God called her to serve. Deborah fully trusted in God, so much so that she risked her life going to battle to wrestle, in God's name, with the enemy.

We Are at War

We, also, are up against an enemy that goes by many names. Methodists describe Satan as "the spiritual forces of wickedness" in the world.[2] We are more vulnerable to this enemy when we try to go it alone. In fact, Satan loves when we wrestle with each other in ways that cause division and harm the church. Satan loves when we put other things before our love of God and our neighbors. God created us to need one another and work together so that we would never have to fight the enemy alone.

In this scripture passage, we see that God called both Deborah and Barak so that together they could defeat their common enemy. God called the Israelites to fight the Canaanites and defeat their king, and in no time Deborah went from a desk job to the front lines. We can presume that she was not trained in combat, but Barak, a general in Israel's army, was. Through Barak's leadership, God would accomplish this feat. But Barak wanted more assurance, so he asked Deborah to help because they were going up against Sisera's powerful army. The Canaanites had advanced weapons, due mainly to their iron chariots, which were virtually undefeatable.

There is no wonder that Barak told Deborah in so many words, "There is no way I am going to fight Sisera without you!" Barak recognized that God was working through Deborah and that she possessed wisdom and strength. When Barak told Deborah that she needed to go too, she immediately responded, "I will surely go with you" (Judg 4:9).

Deborah supported Barak by agreeing to accompany him on this dangerous quest to overthrow the king of Canaan. And before the Israelites went into battle, Deborah further encouraged Barak by telling him that "the LORD [was] indeed going out before [him]" so he would have nothing to worry about (v. 14). Barak led the battle at Mount Tabor. Soon, Sisera's army saw the ten thousand Israelites coming, and their nine hundred iron chariots sprang into action. Can you imagine how terrifying it must have been to see that many iron chariots and their horses coming for the Israelites?

Judges 4:15 tells us that God "threw Sisera and all his chariots and army into a panic." This panic was heightened by a storm that God had brought that trapped the many chariots in the mud. Interestingly these chariots were useless after encountering the simplest of things . . . water. Just as God made a way for the Israelites through the waters of the Red Sea, and again through the waters of the Jordan River, God used water to save the Israelites.

There Are Always Iron Chariots

We all have iron chariots in our lives. We create our own defenses to protect ourselves from any perceived threat. We build up walls to keep others out, thinking if only they knew us they would not like us. Or maybe our walls are built to protect us from getting hurt after experiencing deep pain. Sometimes we build walls around others, judging them before we get to know them. No matter why we build these defenses, they weigh us down, and they do not allow us to receive support from the body of Christ.

God tears down these iron chariots, these perceived safety nets, so that we can be washed by God's grace. Letting go of our defense systems can be scary, but to be in mission or ministry with others we must also be authentic and vulnerable. When we really share who we are, then others feel comfortable sharing who God has created them to be. This is how we build up the body of Christ when we enter into relationships with one another.

Sisera had been quite successful with his iron chariots up until this day. Now that his iron chariots were stuck in the mud and useless, Sisera had no choice but to abandon ship. When he did, he was by himself and vulnerable, and this was the beginning of the end for Sisera. The Israelites trusted God, did their part bravely, and worked together. In the leadership of Deborah and Barak, we see that God used the gifts of each to save the people.

It's All about Relationships

When God calls us to serve, we never know where we will end up. But one thing is certain: doing the work of the Lord means that we will be working with God's people, because doing the work of God always happens in community. The truth is, ministry is all about relationships. It is through the relationships we build that we can do the most effective ministry for Christ. As we all know, relationships can be complicated, yet they are also a means of grace in our lives as others reflect the love and grace of God to us.

As many of the judges and prophets from the Old Testament experienced, caring for God's people can be frustrating. Often, congregation members are in many different places spiritually and personally, and it can be hard to move forward into God's mission together. At other times joy is evident as people become passionate about using their gifts for the Lord. The key is finding the gifts of the people with whom you serve and inviting them to use their gifts in ways that are life-giving.

As you find yourself in mission and ministry, God will also use you and the body of Christ as instruments to bring about God's salvation. I am so thankful to God for the many people I have met throughout my life that I never would have met without God and the church. God's greatest gift to us is Jesus Christ, but I would argue that God's second greatest gift is the church. In the context of the community of God, we get to carry out Christ's ministry in the world. God worked through Deborah, a judge and prophetess, and Barak, the army commander, to bring freedom to God's people. This scripture reminds us that God will equip and empower us to lead in any situation. We see that God does this by providing other people to help us along the way.

Complex and Blessed, Broken and Beautiful

At my first appointment I realized that my idea of ministry was idealistic and naïve. I was excited about serving the local church, and I assumed that everyone would be able to work together and we could make decisions quickly to do the things that God had called us to do. I quickly found this was not the case.

I will never forget the first finance meeting I attended where people argued with one another and were disrespectful to each other.

CHAPTER 5

In fact, I was appalled. Looking back at this time, I think it was in this moment that I finally had the much-needed realization that church people are just people. They are not perfect. We strive to do God's work, but we live in a broken world with broken people. Due to sin, we will always find brokenness in the church; but that does not mean that God cannot work through imperfect people. In fact, this is where God does God's best work. God calls all of us who are so uniquely different to work together to build up the kingdom of God on earth.

> How might God use our brokenness to heal others?

I have always loved the apostle Paul's description of the body of Christ. In 1 Corinthians 12:14 he says: "Indeed, the body does not consist of one member but of many." In other words, we cannot be the hands and feet of Jesus in the world by ourselves. We need many hands, many feet, many minds, and many souls. For years I thought if I just worked hard enough, or if I were faithful enough, I could move the church in the direction I thought it needed to go. God taught me that it is not up to me to move the church in any direction; that is the work of the Holy Spirit. God reminded me that my job was to name how the Holy Spirit was working, to identify the needs of the community, and then to discern with the church body how we were called to serve together.

After going to my third church placement, I finally learned that when you walk into a ministry or mission setting, you must realize you are walking into a place of corporate history; a lot of things have happened before you got there. Each person has their own faith outlook and ideas about the way ministry should happen. Coming into a new ministry setting is like coming into a new family. It will take you a while to get oriented. It will take the church a while to get used to you. Eventually you will learn who the leadership is along with the history of the church. You will learn who you can rely on and who is acting from a place of hurt or fear. In fact, most pastors don't do really great ministry until they have been three to five years in the same place, because this is how long it takes to establish relationships and trust with God's people. Twelve years in, and after serving five churches (one appointment as a three-point charge), I expect to wrestle with others spiritually, theologically, and personally. This is who we are as humans. We are complex and blessed, broken and beautiful.

Holy Wrestling

In answering God's call, you will find yourself wrestling with others. Some people, even those close to you, may doubt your call. This can feel very hurtful, but just know many people are fearful of their loved ones being in ministry because they have seen the underbelly of the church. They may have experienced judgment, hypocrisy, or abuse from a community that was supposed to love them.

Another way you may find yourself wrestling with others is when they ask you why you think God is calling you. At the beginning of answering God's call, it can be difficult to find the words to explain why you are feeling led to serve. Sometimes family members will ask you this question out of concern. They may realize if you commit your life to God that they may not see you as often, you may have to move to a different location, or your relationship with them may change.

Whatever the reason, in answering God's call there will be times when you find yourself wrestling with others. This can also happen when people question your leadership. We know that Moses really suffered because of all the times the Israelites questioned his leadership. He was gone a short time, and they built a golden calf to worship (Exod 32:4). We know a lot of the prophets shared his sentiments.

In this journey of discernment, you must be prepared because people will question your call and your leadership. When someone questions your call, it is yet another opportunity to share your story and the affirmation you have found from others as you have practiced mission or ministry. When people question your leadership, it is an opportunity to hear what is on their hearts and where their concerns are coming from. It is always good to be held accountable, but so many concerns from others come from other places that have nothing to do with you or your ministry setting. You must be confident in your call and your gifts to be able to move forward and do the Lord's work. Deborah was an incredible example of someone who was able to work with others to do God's work.

> Name two of your greatest strengths and your greatest weakness.

Leaning on the Strength of Others

The key to answering God's call is to be able to identity our own strengths and weaknesses. Sometimes this can be a difficult process. For some, it is hard to name strengths. For others, it is difficult to name weaknesses. Yet the better we know ourselves, the better we can minister. If you haven't already, I challenge you to take a personality test or spiritual gifts inventory. Whether you take the Enneagram test or StrengthFinders or another assessment, I encourage you to discuss the results with your pastor, a close friend, or a mentor.

Discerning God's call is a wonderful opportunity for self-discovery. It is also important for all of us to understand why we react the way we do to various situations. One way to think about this is by using Bowen's Family Systems Theory, the "theory of human behavior that views the family as an emotional unit and uses systems thinking to describe the units' complex interactions."[3] In other words, our family of origin affects our development and the way we respond to others. So many things go into making us who we are today. God knows us best, but it is very important for us to spend the time getting to know ourselves. Also, we change and evolve over time, so it is important to continue to take these assessments so we can continue to practice good self-awareness. When we know ourselves well, we are better able to get ourselves out of the way and respond thoughtfully to the needs of others.

In ministry and mission we must play to our strengths and be honest about our gifts. Now, this does not mean that we should not try to grow in key areas. What it *does* mean is that, in the areas in which we are weak, we can ask others to step in or lead the way. This is how we can all use our gifts and build up the body of Christ. We should never be afraid to ask for help appropriately when we feel that we are struggling.

We Do Not Have to Do Everything

Help is always available if only we are willing to ask for it. Pastors and missionaries get in trouble when they try to do everything by themselves. Sometimes it can feel that you are the only person for the job, but I promise you God has given to us the gift of other people for a reason. When you try to do everything by yourself, you may become burned out and bitter. If you find yourself feeling overwhelmed or depressed as you journey with God's people, don't be afraid to ask for help. You are not alone. God is with you, and the body of Christ will support you.

We Go Together

When Barak said, "If you will go with me, I will go" (Judg 4:8), he reminds us that we go out to serve God together. Jesus also sent out his disciples in pairs as they went to serve (Luke 10:1). Barak knew he needed Deborah that day. He needed her God-given wisdom. He needed her moral support and a visual reminder that God was with him. Deborah needed Barak, someone who was skilled in combat and who could protect her on the battlefield. God calls us to go out together so that no one gets left behind.

When we go forward together for God's glory, this also means that we are called to share the gifts that we see in other people. We are called to wrestle with others as they wrestle with God's calling upon their lives. We serve God effectively when, like Deborah, we can recognize God's movement. How are you able to recognize the movement of God in your life or the lives of others? When is the last time you affirmed the gifts of someone in the church community? Our gifts from God are to be celebrated and used to glorify God. If you feel God is calling you to a particular ministry or mission, please share that so your pastor can celebrate that with you. Like Barak, we, too, have been prepared to serve, but we need help from the body of Christ to be able to live fully into God's call upon our lives.

God's Beautiful Tapestry

When I was serving my second church, I found myself serving way out of my comfort zone and deeply in need of the gifts of others. My church was between youth pastors; and as the associate pastor, I offered to take on the youth program. I must admit that youth ministry is not my gift. I love working with youth, but I felt I did not have many of the gifts needed to make the program a success. It took a long time to find someone else to fill this important position. In the meantime I led the weekly youth programs with the help of volunteers and did a lot of planning for our upcoming annual retreat. By the grace of God, we were able to hire someone about two weeks before the retreat. This was Ansley. Ansley was thrown into her new role by leading a massive retreat with forty-five youth and their mentors.

Instead of feeling overwhelmed by such a large task, Ansley came in passionately. Her love for God and the youth were contagious. Like Deborah, Ansley had fire in her belly, which was fueled by her deep desire for the youth to learn and understand Scripture and embody their faith. She had so many gifts for youth ministry and made all the things look easy that had seemed so difficult to me. She was able to discern the needs of each youth and meet them where they were. To say I was thankful for her in that moment is an understatement. Today I get to call Ansley one of my best friends, and I consult her regularly about life and ministry.

Ansley is one of my accountability partners. Part of living in the family of Christ is that we are called to hold one another accountable and encourage each other. We need people to keep asking us hard questions as we are on the journey of discernment. We need people to pray for us. We need people to ask us, "How is it with your soul?" as John Wesley, the founder of the Methodist denomination, did at his weekly small group meetings.[4] We need people to celebrate our gifts and grieve with us on our difficult days.

God gives us the gift of other people to teach us things we cannot learn ourselves. And, as we grow, we also wrestle together. Through the gifts of others, our worldview is expanded. We see people embody their faith in ways that we would never dream or imagine, yet we feel blessed to witness it. In answering God's call, we will wrestle with others, but this wrestling is not all difficult.

In our wrestling with others, God reminds us who we are and who we are called to be. We get to see the beautiful tapestry, God's gifts at work in the body of Christ. Others sometimes challenge us, but instead of feeling defeated by these encounters, we can come away stronger and with a deeper relationship with another person. I am now thankful when people bring their concerns to me. A mutual conversation grounded in respect and full of holy listening only brings us all closer together as we can more deeply understand who we are serving alongside. Holy listening happens when we truly listen to what the other person is saying instead of thinking about how we will respond. Just as in wrestling with God, through wrestling with others we are changed forever.

The Rules of Wrestling and Keeping Boundaries

Wrestling with others happened in the early church. Paul wrote letter after letter to various congregations because they were having a hard time being faithful and getting along. When we wrestle with others on the journey of discernment and self-discovery, we must have good boundaries and a plan for self-care. So many pastors are self-sacrificial; it is in their DNA. They feel called to help people so much that they are willing to sacrifice their emotional, physical, and spiritual health in the process. Burned-out pastors cannot preach life to those they serve. To plan for a ministry with longevity, it is important to have good boundaries and self-care practices from the beginning.

> In what ways do you care for yourself?

Having good boundaries means that you do not let other people control your life. You have a start time and quitting time each day. You remove toxic people from leadership positions as you can, and you stand up for your own needs and the needs of your staff and leadership. Having good boundaries means there is a rhythm to your ministry and mission. You may have seasons that are busier than others, but you take the time after particularly busy seasons to rest. It is important to have good boundaries as a pastor because, in doing so, you set an example for your congregation.

Having healthy boundaries also protects other people. As a pastor, it is up to you to protect your leaders. This means that you do not have unrealistic expectations of others and that you encourage your leaders to take care of themselves. It means that part of your leadership is doing spiritual practices together and that you are regularly checking on others and holding them accountable to the ways in which they have named for themselves to grow.

Practicing self-care is the way you can keep your boundaries. Keep a good calendar and do not overschedule yourself. Take one day of sabbath each week, and start and end your day with prayer or another spiritual discipline. Check in with your colleagues and remain connected. Do not be afraid to ask for help; and, above all, remain rooted in your faith. Surround yourself with those who challenge and encourage you and those who hold you accountable. These holistic practices will allow you to continue to practice ministry year in and year out.

Allow others to use their gifts for God, and wrestle fairly with them. We reflect the face of God more fully when we all work together. Take your time in making big decisions as a church, and allow each voice to be heard. Always allow room for the Holy Spirit to move, and help others to see all the ways that God is working in their lives and in the life of the church. Keep an ear out for how God is calling others, and tell them when you recognize their gifts. And, beloved church, do not be afraid to wrestle with others as you further discern your call. In so doing, you will grow in your own leadership and come to know the gifts of the body of Christ.

Wrestling with Others Spotlight: Rev. Dr. Tammy Williams

My most influential teacher during seminary was Rev. Dr. Tammy Williams. She taught the class "Black Church in America" at Duke Divinity School. She introduced me to the work of Miroslav Volf and made it her mission to teach her students about the sins committed against African Americans. Although I loved her class, I also had a reverent fear each time I entered her classroom.

The class size was small, and Professor Tammy would call on each of us and ask us deep theological questions. Even though I did the reading, I often felt unprepared for the questions she asked me. It was not an easy class, and Professor Tammy expected a lot from her students, but I respected her for that. She knew how to draw the best out of each person, and she expected our best. Professor Tammy had a way of cutting through any surface-level conversation and called us to go deeper into our understanding of God and the church. She cared about her students, and that is why she pushed us all to wrestle with God, ourselves, and one another.

During this class my eyes were opened to my own white privilege and to the struggles going on all around me due to race, many of which I was unaware. Professor Tammy taught us that people of faith do not stand by idly in complicity. It is because of her that every time I serve on a board or agency I ask, "Who else do we need to ask to serve? Whose voice do we need to hear that we may not have yet considered?" Even though I wrestled a lot with myself during Professor Tammy's class, she taught me how to wrestle with others in ways that are fair, just, and faithful. I will always be thankful for the lesson that she instilled within me: that we must understand the past to participate in God's ministry of justice in the present and future. Although Tammy has now gone on to glory, her legacy and impact will live on.

Celebrating God's Victory

In Judges 5, Deborah and Barak sang a song recounting God's salvation in their lives. Many scholars believe that this is the "one of the oldest compositions in the Old Testament, perhaps dating to the twelfth century BCE" and that this was a "victory hymn."[5] Deborah and Barak gave God all the glory for the victory. We know from the Gospels that through Jesus Christ we find victory over sin and death and the enemy. We see through the resurrection of Jesus Christ that death and sin have been defeated. We are called to give thanks to God each day that God gives us the Holy Spirit, as together we continue to be called to fight against the forces of evil in the world. God will go before us, and God will be with us as we continue to wrestle with ourselves and with God's call.

PRAY

Wrestle with me, God, when I am fearful of confrontation. Wrestle with me when others doubt my call and my leadership. Wrestle with me when the trajectory of my life changes to fulfill your will. Wrestle with me when I am called to deal with difficult people. Help me to celebrate the gifts of the diversity of the body of Christ. Help me to practice holy listening and to be able to recognize you in all the conversations I have. Send us forth together to do your work. Amen.

REFLECT

1. Why do you suppose Deborah went with Barak? Why would Barak ask her in the first place?
2. Who is a difficult person for you to work with?
3. Reflect on your strengths and weaknesses. How are you like and unlike your family?
4. How is it with your soul on this journey of discernment?
5. How have others helped you discern God's call?

LISTEN

"How Beautiful" by Twila Paris
https://www.youtube.com/watch?v=8n5uXHE8b78

JOURNAL

Take one of the following assessments: StrengthFinders, Enneagram, or Spiritual Gifts Inventory, and journal about the results. Share these findings with your pastor, trusted friend, or mentor.

6
Wrestling with Detours
ESTHER

When they told Mordecai what Esther had said, Mordecai told them to reply to Esther, "Do not think that in the king's palace you will escape any more than all the other Jews. For if you keep silence at such a time as this, relief and deliverance will rise for the Jews from another quarter, but you and your father's family will perish. Who knows? Perhaps you have come to royal dignity for just such a time as this." Then Esther said in reply to Mordecai, "Go, gather all the Jews to be found in Susa, and hold a fast on my behalf, and neither eat nor drink for three days, night or day. I and my maids will also fast as you do. After that I will go to the king, though it is against the law; and if I perish, I perish." Mordecai then went away and did everything as Esther had ordered him. (Esth 4:12-17)

ESTHER MAY NOT have known it, but she was about to be an agent of new life for her people. Before Esther became queen, she was an orphan who had been taken in by her cousin, Mordecai. He cared for her, and when he saw an opportunity for her to have a better life, he encouraged her to go into the world of the king and the

CHAPTER 6

palace. She caught the king's eye, and it seemed she would be taken care of for life. She even became the queen, but she was living a lie. She had been instructed by Mordecai to hide her identity as a Jew. She was not living fully into the person God had called her to be. Scholars tell us that "Mordecai . . . recommended this strategy of chameleon-like malleability."[1]

I think we can all relate to Mordecai's sentiment for Esther. He wanted her to blend in so that she could continue to survive and thrive. Everyone wants to blend in. Sometimes we are like Esther, and we try to hide our identity from others; we try to hide that we have been called by God for a specific purpose. I've known people who have tried to hide their call, and even their Christianity, but doing this usually causes even more wrestling within their soul. Perhaps they are trying to hide because they do not want to be perceived as different from colleagues and friends. Or perhaps they don't want to have to prove to others that God has called them.

> In what ways have you tried to blend in? How did that work out?

God has taught me that the life of ministry and mission calls us not to blend in. In fact, many times God calls us to stick out like a sore thumb as we speak against cultural norms to remind others about who God is and who God is calling us to be. As you answer God's call, you may feel tempted to turn away instead of walking toward God. Sometimes we all want to be like a chameleon and live simple lives. I admit I do have thoughts sometimes about how nice it would be to have a nine-to-five job. Through Esther's story, God reminds us that in the detours we find God and a way forward.

Esther had a decision to make: she could live on easy street, or she could take a detour to save her people. This very action could cost her life, but the lives of her people were in jeopardy. The agent of death in this passage of scripture was the evil Haman, a royal official whose goal was to sentence all the Jews to death. Mordecai found out about Haman's plot and went to great effort to get this vital message to Esther.

Mordecai's words, "Perhaps you have come to royal dignity for just such a time as this" spurred Esther to action (Esth 4:14b). Esther realized that she would not be able to do this important work by herself; she needed the help of her faith family. She formed a plan of action: "Go, gather together all the Jews to be found in Susa, and hold a fast on my behalf, and neither eat nor drink for three days, night or day. I and my maids will also fast as you do. After that I will go to the king, though it is against the law; and if I perish, I perish" (v. 16).

Through Mordecai's invitation to this detour, Esther became the person God was calling her to be. I wonder what would have happened if Mordecai had never spoken these words to her? Would the outcome have been the same? We all need a brother or sister in Christ like Mordecai, someone who is committed deeply to their faith and invites us to participate in God's ministry of salvation.

Sometimes we, too, need to hear words such as these from a trusted friend or family member. This is where we find affirmation in our call: when someone tells us something we already know about ourselves, we are spurred to move forward to follow God's plan for our lives. When we know that people believe in us and our gifts, then we, too, can take immediate action.

In that moment, Esther realized that her position of power was not enough. She was willing to risk her life, but she knew she had to do more. Together, she and her people fasted and prayed for God to save them. They put their full trust in God. Through Esther's courageous action of coming before the king, God responded and saved God's people.

As we encounter detours in our lives, we must discern who is leading us there. Are we going a different way because of our own desires, or are we following God in a new direction? God has given us the gift of free will, and we are charged to use it as we make decisions about our next steps. Remember, our lives are full of detours—opportunities for God to teach us more and equip us for the next task.

CHAPTER 6

Praying for a Way Forward

I encourage you to take the time to pray to God about where God is leading you in your discernment journey. Just as Esther prayed and called her people to pray, we are also called to pray, especially when we find ourselves at a crossroads. Ask God, "Which way would you have me go?" Or "What should I do, God?" As we are confronted with the detours of life, we wrestle with God to know which way God is calling us to go.

You Are Called for This Time

Like Esther, we are called to act in the midst of suffering and tragedy. Now, more than at any other time in history, people of faith are called to speak out against injustice and oppression. We can no longer be silent when God's people are being treated unfairly and unjustly. We, like Esther, are called "for just such a time as this." Mordecai's statement shows that Esther was called to take immediate action. Instead of waiting around or making excuses, now is the time to act. Now is the time to decide about where God is leading you next. We all make these decisions as we continue the process of discernment. And in our blessed wrestling we, like Esther, all encounter detours.

Dealing with Detours

Have you ever been driving down the road having a lovely day and then you see a dreaded detour sign? Some detours are not a big deal; we simply change lanes, and we are past them. At other times, detours take us far out of our comfort zones, and we find ourselves on back roads we have never seen before. You cannot plan for a detour.

What detours have you encountered in your life?

Detours are caused by many factors in our lives. Sometimes we get in our own way; we make excuses for why we cannot answer God's call and convince ourselves that answering is impossible. Sometimes other people get in our way; the expectations and obligations that we feel to our family and friends can steer us away from answering God's call. And sometimes God takes us on these detours to show us a different way—a way that we never even knew existed. My experience is that, just when I think I am being detoured, God shows me I am exactly where I am supposed to be.

At the beginning of a detour, we are unable to see the way God is leading us, but once we follow God, we can see just far enough ahead to realize that God is calling us to use our gifts to serve. If we trust where God is leading, we will end up serving in places we never imagined and yet were supposed to be all along.

In Isaiah 43:1-3 God reminds us why we should always place our trust in God:

> But now thus says the LORD,
>   he who created you, O Jacob,
>   he who formed you, O Israel:
> Do not fear, for I have redeemed you;
>   I have called you by name, you are mine.
> When you pass through the waters, I will be with you;
>   and through the rivers, they shall not overwhelm you;
> when you walk through fire you shall not be burned,
>   and the flame shall not consume you.
> For I am the LORD your God,
>   the Holy One of Israel, your Savior.

In this scripture we remember that God created us and loves us and that God will see us through the fires and floods of our lives and bring us out on the other side. Through faith, God will continue to save us. Why waste our time on fear when we can spend our time being excited about what God is calling us to do next?

If I were to name the number one reason that people do not answer God's call, it would be fear. Fear of how their lives will

> God is Lord of the future. God is our friend. We need not fear.

change. Fear of surrender. Fear of the reaction of family and friends. Fear that they are not qualified or not good enough. Fear that maybe they misinterpreted what God was saying to them. It is normal to feel afraid to answer God's call, but we cannot stay in this place of fear. Eventually we must take action and move forward in God's call.

We Serve a God Who Keeps Promises

I am thankful that we are not the only ones who have had trouble putting our full trust in God. Throughout the Bible, there were others who admitted they had a hard time trusting in God when they found themselves in a season of detours. For instance, the Israelites experienced detour after detour, and they let Moses know they were not happy with his leadership. God promised them land, and they wanted to find the Promised Land right then. All along the way, God showed them that God was providing for them.

God made water spring forth from rocks. God provided manna from heaven. God moved whole bodies of water twice so that they could cross over safely. Through it all, God was with them, leading them forward, calling them to action. God continued to show the Israelites that new life was all around them if only they would look for it.

Perception Matters

Our outlook on life is affected by our perception. Do we perceive God's calling to be a detour or an opportunity? Instead of feeling inconvenienced and overwhelmed, celebrate that God is calling you to try something new. In the perceived detours of our lives, we find a new way forward. God will lead us out of the detours of this life.

Throughout the Gospels, we see the disciples following Jesus from place to place. I believe there had to be a type A disciple who asked Jesus each day about the day's itinerary. Often Jesus and his disciples would plan to go to one place and end up going a totally different way (usually for their own safety). Although many believers helped to house the disciples, they still experienced detours as they were doing the ministry of Jesus Christ.

As Jesus sent his disciples out into mission and ministry, he instructed them:

"Whatever town or village you enter, find out who in it is worthy, and stay there until you leave. As you enter the house, greet it. If the house is worthy, let your peace come upon it; but if it is not worthy, let your peace return to you. If anyone will not welcome you or listen to your words, shake off the dust from your feet as you leave that house or town." (Matt 10:11-14)

Jesus prepared the disciples for detours. He called them to rely on the body of Christ, but he also gave them permission to go another way when they encountered people who weren't interested in hearing the good news of Christ. As you answer God's call, prepare for detours, prepare to wrestle with God and others as you also proclaim the good news of Christ.

Even through Pandemics

Many people have asked me if anyone still feels called to ministry during this season. As I write this book, we have just come through the year 2020—the year of the global COVID-19 pandemic, the height of racial injustice, and even murder hornets.[2] The year when churches closed their doors and wearing masks became our new normal. The year when people were more worried about simply surviving than their spiritual growth and discipleship. Here is my answer: yes, now more than ever, people need to hear the good news of Jesus Christ.

Like Esther, perhaps you have been called for such a time as this. You can be an agent of Christ's resurrection in the world today. Ask yourself: "What is stopping me from answering God's call?" Are you fearful? Do you feel that you have too much to lose? Instead of seeing signs of resurrection all around you, you may be caught up in grief: the grief of how you thought your future would look; the grief of opportunities that you refused so that you could say yes to God; or, possibly, grief over the loss of a family member, partner, spouse, important friend, or mentor. Grief can stop us in our tracks and leave us unable to answer God's call.

Gideon's Detour

The good news for our lives is that God will continue to call us even when we are not ready to place our full trust in God. Gideon had a hard time trusting in God's plan for his life. God called Gideon to serve during a time of oppression for his people. Gideon was in hiding, hanging out in caves so as not to be killed by the Midianites; but he could not hide from God. God sought him out and called him to do something new.

The story of Gideon in Judges 6 reminds us that, even when we may be in a season of detours, God provides signs for us that God is at work. In the Bible, many times signs are the start of something new—usually a relationship with God. God used a rainbow as a sign of the covenant with Noah, the start of a new relationship and promise. God used tablets to show the Israelites how God was calling them to live in relationship.

Throughout the Bible, God uses tangible things to show God's people that they have been called out by God to participate in God's saving action in the world. Like Esther, God called Gideon to help save his people. Like most call stories in the Bible, Gideon did not respond immediately to God's request and had to be convinced that God was in fact calling him. He had a couple of reservations: (1) How could he trust a God who had allowed his people to experience oppression? (2) Did he have the skill set that was necessary for the task?

So Gideon made God prove that he was indeed being called to serve. The angel of the Lord had already given Gideon one sign: a food offering prepared by Gideon disappeared in a flash of fire. But the first sign wasn't enough for Gideon. He asked God to perform a simple task, to make dew appear on his fleece and not the ground. And God did. But this second sign was still not enough for Gideon, so the next morning he asked for there to be dew on the ground and not on the fleece. Again, God gave him this third sign. Now he would have to rely on God as the Living Water. From this point forward, Gideon continued to prepare for battle with the Midianites.

> Why do we ask God for a sign? What does that say about us and our relationship with God?

You see, God was preparing Gideon for a time to face and defeat his enemies. Isn't this what God is preparing us for every day? God prepares us as we face the forces of wickedness in the world today. In our humanity we require signs from God to know that we are on the right track. We require assurance and need encouragement to stay on the right path as we celebrate that God is with us. God does not just give us signs and then leave us alone. God is with us and helps us fight our battles against sin through our faith in Jesus Christ and the power of the Holy Spirit.

> Where do you need assurance and encouragement?

Communion: The Great Course Corrector

Sometimes we take detours because we are lost. During those times, we need a course corrector. One of the most beautiful signs we have that God is with us is the sacrament of Holy Communion. Through this "sign-act," we enter the story of God and get on God's path for us. God created us, then we fell into sin. Through Jesus Christ we are saved, and we continue to grow in discipleship through the Holy Spirit. That is God's path for us as we strive for what John Wesley called "Christian perfection"; what he described as "perfect love of God and neighbor."[3] Through the simple actions of holding up the bread and wine, we see Christ's body broken and blood spilled out so that we can truly live and have everlasting life.

Communion is a centering sacrament, one that can put us back on the right path. No matter what is going on in our lives, everything is pushed aside as we participate in Communion, the great course corrector. When we take Communion, we acknowledge that we are all sinners in need of God's divine grace; we all get lost and distracted. We all come to Christ's table broken and leave full of the Holy Spirit and God's grace. Communion is a sign from God, or as John Wesley would say, a "means of grace"[4] in which we take a foretaste of the kingdom of God and our hungry souls are thereby nourished by God. Often during Communion, God gives me the assurance that I am exactly where I am supposed to be.

When You Are on a Detour, Focus on God

Becoming queen came with the danger that Esther would completely lose her Jewish identity.[5] It took a crisis for Esther to go back to her roots. It took a crisis for Esther to remember who she was and how God had given her the opportunity to save her people. Even during the detours in your life, stay focused on God, and God will lead you forward.

> What are some ways to keep you focused on God and where God is leading?

One of my most loved Bible stories is in Matthew 14:22-32, when Peter walks on water to make his way to Jesus. Peter always gets a bad rap for not trusting in Christ in this moment, but we must give him credit. He was the only disciple who got out of the boat. We, like the other disciples, want to stay in the boat. We want to go back to the dry land and kiss the ground. We want a life jacket, at least, so that if we start sinking we can save ourselves. But Peter knew who he was and who Jesus is. When you say yes to God's call, you will follow Christ where he is calling you to go.

Peter knew that Jesus was the Son of God. He knew this with every fiber of his being, yet when he broke eye contact with Jesus, he started sinking. He got distracted, perhaps by having second thoughts and realizing exactly what he was actually doing. At first everything was going well. As long as Peter was focused on Jesus, he was fine. But when he started looking around at his surroundings, his fear betrayed him. He started to sink. And his fear betrayed him again later in the courtyard and led him to deny Jesus.

Sometimes we are like Peter. Surely just being a disciple was a detour from their previous lives—the lives they and their families expected. We believe in Christ with our whole being, but we get distracted by all the things going on around us. These distractions can take our eyes off Christ and cause us to veer off course and get lost. What is distracting you from answering God's call? Is it family, friends, a career that you feel comfortable in, or worrying about the unknown? Keep your eyes on Christ and follow.

This past summer I had the pleasure of hosting an intern from Wesley Theological Seminary. I knew Susan from the previous church I served. At that time she voiced a call to ordained ministry and decided to go to seminary. But during seminary, Susan experienced a detour. Her beloved grandfather died suddenly, which left her in shock and deep grief. Her grief combined with her many obligations caused her to feel overwhelmed by the stress of school, and her anxiety was at an all-time high. So with only one semester left, she decided to take a semester off from school. She wondered if she would ever return.

God continued to work on Susan as the Holy Spirit whispered to her, "Go back to school." During that season in her life, Susan was blessed to work as the children's director at a United Methodist Church. There, they celebrated her gifts for ministry. She remembered her call and was encouraged to return to school. One day I received a phone call from Susan out of the blue.

Susan needed a favor. The internship she needed to graduate had fallen through. She needed somewhere to serve as soon as possible! God was giving me another chance to support Susan. After consulting with my leadership team, I said yes, and Susan spent the summer with us discerning and growing in her call. She expressed a clear call back to the children and family ministry that she loves. That same year, she graduated and received her master of divinity degree from Wesley Theological Seminary. Susan could have let the circumstances of her life detour her in a completely different direction. She could have given up, but God kept calling her back to the path. She kept her eyes on Jesus, and God called her to act and move forward in her call. I cannot wait to see where Susan will end up, and I am so excited for the churches in which she will serve in the future.

In life we have a choice. Do we give up, or do we keep fighting? Do we accept our role, as Esther did, to follow where God leads? This is what wrestling with God is all about. God calls, we answer. God calls again, we don't answer. God calls us again and again until we are ready to put our full trust in God and act. In the detours of life, God give us opportunities to use our difficult experiences to help other people.

Wrestling with Detours Spotlight: Angie Williams

I met Angie when I was a young adult. At that time she worked for the Virginia Conference as the director of ministries with young people. Angie was a young adult herself. She was passionate and warm, and she genuinely cared about building relationships with as many people as she could. Serving in this capacity was a detour from the way she grew up. In her family of origin she was taught that women were not leaders, but Angie was a natural and gifted leader.

Angie experienced a call to serve God as a youth. With tears she preached on her youth Sunday, not knowing why she was crying. Years later she realized her tears came as a sign that God was affirming her call through the power and presence of the Holy Spirit and the body of Christ. At that time Angie could not put into words what she was feeling; but she listened to God, and since that time she has served God in so many ways. Angie describes that her passion for helping the most vulnerable children has been the "driving force" in her life "both professionally and personally."

Angie lives her life holistically as worship to God. Professionally she has chosen a career to help vulnerable children, and personally she has adopted two girls from the same biological family who were in foster care. As Angie took on this new role as a mother, she found God had placed a new call on her life. After her oldest daughter graduated and moved out, Angie really wrestled with God.

Angie was heartbroken that her daughter was struggling so much with her past, and not even Angie's love could heal her pain. During a drive to see her daughter, Angie felt God speak to her and give her a vision in what Angie called her "burning bush" moment. Angie said, "During that drive, which I will never ever forget as long as I live, I felt God speak to me in my spirit and give me a vision that I would become part of a movement and a future solution for kids like mine whose families were experiencing economic and relational poverty." Through her love for her daughters, Angie was called to go in a new direction.

Again, Angie wrestled with God. She knew what God had called her to do but grew impatient in waiting for this moment to be realized. Then, on a work trip to Michigan three years later, Angie had another "burning bush" moment. At a conference at the Open Table, Angie's call was affirmed again. She said, "I knew this was what I had been searching for.... I knew it was the answer to change the trajectory of

CHAPTER 6

kids like my own. . . . I knew this was the movement to which God had called me to address economic and relational poverty."

Instead of lamenting that she could not start working for this organization immediately, Angie started a "table" with the support of her local church. There she met another young woman who had aged out of the foster-care system. Angie poured herself out to this young woman and was blessed through the relationship they created together. She considers this young woman to be like a third daughter to her. Angie is now the managing director of Open Table, where she works tirelessly every day to seek justice for children who are the most at risk. Angie believes that serving in this role is the deepest, most authentic way for her to live out her discipleship and "the clearest path to human reconciliation that [she has] ever experienced."

Through a detour from the theology of her family of origin, Angie's call was affirmed by the body of Christ, and she was sent out to serve those in need of justice and mercy. Angie still maintains and celebrates a close and beautiful relationship with her family, while she remains confident in her call. Through the wrestling with God in the detours of her life, Angie gained three daughters, four grandchildren, and affirmation in her call with a new sense of purpose.

God can teach us important lessons when we find ourselves in a season of detours, but it is up to us to look for the signs of how God is leading us forward to action. My hope for you is that in this moment you may feel affirmed in your call, that you may have been called for "such a time as this." My prayer for you is that you will be courageous like Esther and Gideon as you keep your heart and mind focused on Christ. Do not lose God in the detours of this life. Look for the signs of new life, and you may have the realization that, in the detours, God prepares us for future ministry.

PRAY

Wrestle with me, God, when I cannot see detours as opportunities to see your ministry of resurrection in my life. Wrestle with me when I am weighed down by the grief of this life and unable to move forward. Wrestle with me when I am not ready to take action. Help me to believe that I, too, have been called "for just such a time as this." Amen.

REFLECT

1. What detours have you taken? Have they stopped you from answering God's call?
2. How did the detours work out? Who supported you? What kind of support do you want?
3. Where have you or someone you know experienced resurrection and new life?
4. How have difficult moments helped you help others?
5. How can you encourage others to respond to God's call upon their lives?

LISTEN

"Thy Will" by Hillary Scott and the Scott Family
https://www.youtube.com/watch?v=Dp4WC_YZAuw

JOURNAL

How do you feel called for "such a time as this"?

7
Wrestling with Obligation
RUTH

But Naomi said, "Turn back, my daughters, why will you go with me? Do I still have sons in my womb that they may become your husbands? Turn back, my daughters, go your way, for I am too old to have a husband. Even if I thought there was hope for me, even if I should have a husband tonight and bear sons, would you then wait until they were grown? Would you then refrain from marrying? No, my daughters, it has been far more bitter for me than for you, because the hand of the LORD has turned against me." Then they wept aloud again. Orpah kissed her mother-in-law, but Ruth clung to her.

So she said, "See, your sister-in-law has gone back to her people and to her gods; return after your sister-in-law." But Ruth said,

"Do not press me to leave you
    or to turn back from following you!
Where you go, I will go;
    where you lodge, I will lodge;
your people shall be my people,
    and your God my God.
Where you die, I will die—

> there will I be buried.
> May the LORD do thus and so to me,
> and more as well,
> if even death parts me from you!"
>
> When Naomi saw that she was determined to go with her, she said no more to her. (Ruth 1:11-18)

Bonds of Obligation, Bonds of Love

In our scripture from the book of Ruth, Naomi was dealing with obligation. She was on her way from Moab, where she had lived, back to her home country to search for food and a place to live after her husband and two sons had died. During this time, women were particularly vulnerable when they did not have a man from their family to protect them and provide for them. Naomi found herself on a journey that day back to Bethlehem (which means "house of bread) because she probably had nowhere else to go and she was hungry. As she walked with her two daughters-in-law, we can imagine that she felt the tension of obligation, and she admitted it. She told these women that they no longer had an obligation to be her family. She freed them from the responsibility of taking care of her, and she told them to go home.

In this selfless action of Naomi, her love for her two daughters-in-law is evident. She knew that their best chance at life would be to find another husband. Without this chance they might not survive, and Naomi wanted what was best for them. She gave them a free choice to leave without guilt and without regret. At first Orpah and Ruth said they would not leave her and that they would return to her home with her. But, after Naomi's persistence in telling them to "turn back," Orpah took this opportunity to say goodbye and leave (Ruth 1:12). Ruth, however, decided to stay with Naomi. The Bible tells us she "clung to her" (v. 14). Just as Jacob clung to God as he was wrestling with God, here we see Ruth cling to Naomi, not out of fear or guilt, but out of love.

Ruth surely realized that Naomi was speaking out of grief and that, if Ruth left, Naomi might not survive on her own. Naomi was in a bad place. She even wanted to change her name to "Mara" (which means "bitterness") to reflect the way she felt toward God (v. 20). Naomi had lost everything; and in trying to rid her daughters-in-law of their obligation, I believe she was simply preparing to die. In her mind she had nothing left to live for. In that moment Ruth realized she had a decision to make. She, too, had the option to walk away and start over afresh. But that day, Ruth showed Naomi that the bonds of family go beyond blood, and the bonds of obligation go beyond legalities. Ruth claimed Naomi as her own and gave her a new purpose for living, reminding Naomi that she had worth, even if she felt worthless.

Ruth fully surrendered herself when she put the needs of Naomi above her own. As a result, instead of choosing death and despair, Naomi chose life—all because her daughter-in-law showed her that she was important and loved. What a powerful example of love and sacrifice!

Like Orpah, we may think it is a lot easier to walk away than to stay and accept an obligation that God has set before us. Like Orpah, we may want to walk away from God's call so that we can gain the success expected for us and named for us by the world. Ruth's decision to stay with Naomi was a difficult one because she was choosing a harder life and she knew it.

To prove her point to Naomi that she was serious about staying, Ruth made an impassioned speech:

"Do not press me to leave you
   or to turn back from following you!
Where you go, I will go;
   where you lodge, I will lodge;
your people shall be my people,
   and your God my God.
Where you die, I will die—
   there will I be buried.

> May the Lord do thus and so to me,
>> and more as well,
> if even death parts me from you!" (Ruth 1:16-17)

Some may read Ruth's speech and say, "Well that's nice, but those are just words." But taking a closer look can give us a deeper understanding of Ruth's words. At that time, "every vow of a widow . . . by which she has bound herself, shall be binding upon her."[1] These powerful words uttered by Ruth were not meant to cheer up Naomi in the moment, but to bind her to Naomi for life.

Ruth 1:16-17 is a popular scripture passage for weddings because this is how Christian commitment looks. In that moment, Ruth reiterated that she and Naomi were still family through the bonds of love. When Ruth bound herself to Naomi, she also made a commitment that she would worship God, the same God that Naomi worshiped. In Ruth's actions of surrender and emptying herself for the sake of Naomi, she found herself full of the promise of having a future with God.

Ruth teaches us that the most important gift that God gives to us (besides Jesus Christ and the Holy Spirit) is the gift of God's people: the community of faith—the church. Discipleship is all about relationships. We formalize our commitment to God in the promises we make when we join the church; that is, we define our obligations. In Mark 12:30-31, Jesus tells us, "'Love the Lord your God with all your heart, and with all your soul, and with all your mind, and with all your strength.' The second is this: 'You shall love your neighbor as yourself.' There is no commandment greater than these." Through our faith in Jesus Christ, we freely choose to obligate ourselves to love God and care for our neighbors. Ruth understood the importance of caring for someone else and preserving life.

Priorities and Obligations

In answering God's call, we all wrestle with obligation, and we can find ourselves wrestling with God when the Holy Spirit reminds us of our obligation to respond to our Creator. We also wrestle with the obligations we have to families and friends. We care deeply about these people, and deep down we want to please them. We want to make sure they are taken care of. Sometimes these obligations are self-imposed or the result of others' expectations and may leave us feeling that we are unable to answer God's call.

Sometimes we feel we are unable to answer God's call because we are caring for a loved one or, perhaps, we are experiencing an illness ourselves. Other times we feel we cannot step away from our current job because it is how we are supporting ourselves or our families. You may be in such a situation, but do not lose heart. You can still live out your call where you are by ministering to those you are with. Living into God's call does not happen in one moment; it is a matter of priorities. It is a choice we make each day to do the things that God calls us to do.

> Who are the most important people in your life? What obligations come with those relationships?

Ecclesiastes 3:1 reminds us, "For everything there is a season, and a time for every matter under heaven." In some seasons of life you are freer to serve in the ways in which you would like. In other busier seasons it may be all you can do to survive; nevertheless, God can use you where you are right now. Do not wait for the perfect circumstances to answer God's call, because perfect circumstances do not exist. There will always be other things and other people who demand your time and attention. Make opening yourself to God a priority; make listening to God a daily practice.

Upholding Obligations

Through the years it has become culturally acceptable to become, as theologian Stanley Hauerwas puts it, "a quivering mass of availability."[2] In other words, we are unable to sit still, and this has become

CHAPTER 7

the norm. The next time you go to the doctor's office, look around the waiting area. To pass the time most people are doing something on their phones or tablets. In Scripture, God calls us to stillness so we can experience God moving in our lives. In Psalm 46:10-11, God tells us:

> "Be still, and know that I am God!
> I am exalted among the nations.
> I am exalted in the earth."
> The LORD of hosts is with us;
> the God of Jacob is our refuge.

God is always calling us to serve, but are we able to faithfully hear the voice of God when we feel weighed down by our obligations?

We currently live in a time when we are separated from one another. Usually community may happen for us only in the workplace or at church on Sunday mornings. Many of us don't know our neighbors, and most of us may not answer the door when strangers knock. This is not the way community was during the time of the Bible. People lived within walking distance of one another and the temple, and neighbors cared for one another. Hospitality was a virtue and obligation and remains so in much of the world. The community shared food and resources, and even took care of strangers (Lev 19:34).

When have you had to let go of an obligation? What obligations weigh you down?

In the Old Testament book of Leviticus, we see how God calls us to live in community. We share in God's ministry of welcome when we share our resources with others; this is mercy in action. We see this embodied in Leviticus 23:22 where God called farmers not to reap their harvest at the edge of their field so the poor or alien could have food and live. The crops at the edge of the field were thought as castoffs; they were smaller since they were farther away from the nitrogen-rich soil in the middle of the field. Yet these cast-off vegetables were agents of life. As it turned out, this practice fed Ruth and Naomi.

God taught the Israelites that everything they had should be used for God's glory. Something they thought was garbage, such as the cast-off crops, could literally save the life of their neighbor. Because of this community of God, people survived during the harsh times when famines came. The community of God was also important in the New Testament. In fact, in Acts 6:1-6 seven men were appointed exclusively to care for widows. In the early church, hospitality was vital. Gatherings of the faithful took place in homes, as there were no church buildings.

The Ties That Bind

Ruth models for us what it means to take part in the community of God. Ruth answered God's call when she told Naomi she would never leave her side. In ministry and mission, we offer ourselves to the communities of faith in which we serve. We are bound to these communities through our commitment to God, and we are obligated to care for those whom God has placed in our care. Yet so often, instead of experiencing joy over this holy responsibility, the weight of the importance of this task can cause us to walk away from ministry all together.

> Who are the people easiest for you to care for? Who are the most difficult?

Caring for God's people is a big responsibility. Just as physicians are tasked to care for their patients' bodies, we, as ministers, are called to care for people's souls. Tending the souls of others is hard work because witnessing the depth of wrestling that others endure can wear on our own souls. Yet, in this holy work of obligation and commitment to God's people, we also get to see how God is at work. We witness as people wrestle with God, being changed and blessed.

In Luke 15, God reminds us why every person in our care is important to God.

> "Which one of you, having a hundred sheep and losing one of them, does not leave the ninety-nine in the wilderness and go after the one that is lost until he finds it? When he has found it, he lays it on his shoulders and rejoices. And when he comes home, he calls together his friends and neighbors, saying to them, 'Rejoice with me, for I have found my sheep that was lost.' Just so, I tell you, there will be more joy in heaven over one sinner who repents than over ninety-nine righteous persons who need no repentance." (vv. 2-7)

As we say yes to God, we, too, are called to go after the one sheep. We are called to find people when they cannot find God. We are called to know the names of all our "sheep" so that we can recognize when someone is missing. We are called to rejoice mightily when one person who was lost has now found God.

In tending to the body of Christ, we will find ourselves changed for the better. Paul understood how we change each other through our faith in God. In 1 Corinthians 12:26 he says, "If one member suffers, all suffer together with it; if one member is honored, all rejoice together with it." Through being part of the body of Christ, we experience one another's valleys and mountaintop experiences. As a pastor or missionary, you are called to feel the experiences of your community; but if you try to take this on without a strong relationship with God and without the support of the faith community, you will falter. While you acknowledge pain and joy and lead the community forward as they grow in their love and knowledge of God, you cannot harbor those feelings. Your boundaries must be in place. This is hard to do, and congregations have high and sometimes unrealistic expectations. While it may be tempting to think you have to do everything yourself, you cannot. To survive in ministry you must enlist the help of others. The community is the body of Christ, and it is the community that seeks the lost and brings home those who have gone astray. It is the community who loves the least and the last.

This holy obligation that we call ministry is a gift from God; this is why pastors hang on even when ministry is difficult and people question our authority and perhaps our salvation. This is why pastors miss meals with their families to answer an important call and reschedule their calendars for a funeral. At the same time, your family is also part of the community of faith. You have obligations to them, and sometimes these obligations of family and church compete and conflict. When you decide to answer God's call, your life is no longer your own. But by offering yourself to God, God will help you set priorities and wrestle with conflicting obligations. God will send people to help you, as God did with Paul. God will help you to live into your limitations and find grace and peace. Do not lament this holy obligation; celebrate it.

> What is an example of conflicting obligations or competing loyalties?

In your ministry you might not always find a spiritual home where you are serving, but I hope you will find a community that celebrates your arrival and affirms your call. However, as a pastor's spouse once told me, there will always be people happy to see you come and happy to see you go. That's just part of it. Yet you will meet the neatest and most inspirational people. You will hear stories that live in your heart for the rest of your life. You will see God move, which will remind you of why you do this sacred work.

Accountability and Support

I could not do this holy work we call ministry without the support of my family, colleagues, and friends. We need one another, and we need accountability and encouragement. During the eighteenth century, there lived a man who was passionate about Christian accountability. His name was John Wesley; he was an Anglican priest and a graduate of Oxford University in England. He was also the founder of a worldwide family of Methodist denominations. Wesley said that we are called to watch over one another's souls.[3] The United Methodist Church was born out of what were effectively these Christian accountability groups. Wesley knew that people would fall away from God between church services, so he set up a system to help people out. He created classes and bands, which were accountability groups.

The purpose of these small groups of ten to twelve people was to meet, confess their sins, pray for each other, and serve the poor and needy. These groups profoundly impacted the lives of all who participated, and they helped the Methodist movement spread like rapid fire. Some questions asked were, "How is it with your soul?" and "Am I consciously or unconsciously creating the impression that I am better than I really am? In other words, am I a hypocrite?"[4] You see, Wesley and the people called Methodists had the same struggles that we have today. They wanted to be good Christians but found it hard to practice their faith on a daily basis; this is why we need each other. Of course, we are always accountable to God, first and foremost, but God has given us the gift of other people to help us learn how to keep practicing our faith. The good news for us is that God calls us to care for each other.

Not Only Clergy

Pastors are not the only ones called to this holy ministry. The moment we profess Jesus Christ as our Savoir, we commit our lives to God and are bound in a covenant (an understanding of our obligations) with God and the faith community. Throughout my life I have been blessed by so many laity (non-clergy) who take this commitment seriously. Recently, my lay leader, Ce, died after a short battle with stage four stomach cancer. Ce was a cheerful servant of the church.

She loved being in God's house and would spend much of her time there. She even had a phone installed in the church so that people would know where to look for her.

Ce prepared the church each Sunday for worship. She adorned the altar carefully with the correct color of parament for the season of the church year. She prepared the elements for Communion and took great joy in holding the Communion cup and saying to others, "the blood of Christ given for you."[5] Ce would preach on occasion and was gifted in her understanding of the Bible. Most of all, Ce viewed her service as her obligation to God and her joy. She did not want accolades; and it wasn't until after her death that we all realized she was not only serving our church, but the community, and at her job as well. I am thankful for Ce's faithful witness of commitment to Christ and her lasting impact on my life.

> Why might it be more difficult for some to keep their obligations than others?

You may be feeling the weight of obligation as you decide whether to pursue ministry or mission. What obligations in your life are holding you back from answering God's call? What obligations of ministry or mission scare you? Ministry is not for the faint of heart, yet when you surrender your life to God, God will sustain you. God will give you renewal and hope and energy to do the work that God has set before you. God will send other people to support you.

In the Old Testament, obligation played out in an exchange. One person would do something, and the other person was obligated to do something in return. This is true in many cultures today. In the book of Leviticus we see this played out in the way that people responded to God's word. God instructed the Israelites to follow the law, and through faith they were obliged to listen to God and act accordingly. In the New Testament, obligation was redefined by Jesus Christ. John 13:14 tells us that Jesus said to the disciples, "So if I, your Lord and Teacher, have washed your feet, you also ought

CHAPTER 7

to wash one another's feet." In this exchange with the disciples, Jesus taught that obligation to God is not just about following the law; it is about caring for our neighbors. And if we take the parable of the Good Samaritan seriously, our neighbors include our enemies and those who are not like us. Paul understood Christ's words when in Romans 1:14 he wrote, "I am a debtor both to Greeks and to barbarians, both to the wise and to the foolish."

God Keeps God's Obligations

Through God's call, Paul knew that he had an obligation to bring all people to God by using his God-given gifts. This holy obligation is not a burden but a beautiful opportunity. Ruth never could have imagined that, in the moment she selflessly gave of herself to Naomi, a chain of events would begin in which she would be part of the lineage of Jesus Christ.[6] Who knows what God will allow you to witness within your lifetime of ministry?

When I was in seminary, I witnessed God's holy obligation upon the life of my fellow classmate. He was from Korea, and he moved his whole family to North Carolina so that he could answer God's call. His English was conversational at best. I first encountered him in the library working on a term paper. He was sitting at a table by himself, surrounded by resources. I left the library for lunch and another class and came back, and he was still there working. In that moment, the Holy Spirit moved in my heart and told me to talk to him. It was not until the next day that I answered this call of the Spirit and found him sitting at the same table, determined to finish his paper.

I introduced myself, and he shared with me what he was working on. In Korean he could beautifully argue the main point of his term paper, but he said his papers took him such a long time to write because he was still learning English. In that moment I knew this man was called by God to this holy work of ministry. He cared so much about doing God's work that he would spend countless hours wrestling, fighting for every word because it was that important.

My trivial concerns of the day seemed meaningless. At least I got to write in my first language. I decided to help my new friend. He would tell me in his own words what he was trying to say, and I helped him string along the words in a contextual manner. Eventually he did not need my help, and he learned English quickly by having to write so much and working so hard each day.

There are people in this life who sacrifice so much to answer God's call. Some leave their home country, as Ruth did, and find themselves in a wilderness of difficultly. Others lose the closeness they once had with their family as they move away in order to answer God's call. It is the obligation that we take on as pastors, this way that God sustains us, that allows us to continue to answer God's call.

In life we have many obligations. Whether our obligation is to our faith, families, friends, careers, or even pets, we cannot let these obligations get in the way of answering God's call. God will help you find a way to fulfill, resolve, or let go of your obligations as you move forward in answering God's call.

Wrestling with Obligation Spotlight: Rev. Rita Callis

The first district pastors' meeting I ever attended was in Newport News, Virginia. I was nervous as I arrived; I knew I was the only young woman in the district. I felt an obligation to represent all young women in ministry. As I entered the meeting, I felt anxiety as I started comparing myself immediately with my other colleagues. But my anxiety faded away when I met Rita Callis. Rita was one of those people who was who she was; she didn't pretend to be someone different. She was confident in the gifts God gave her, and in her I saw a freedom I did not yet possess. Rita was warm, bright, and funny. She sought me out immediately at the meeting and invited me to sit by her. She was able to sense my anxiety at being a newbie, and she broke the ice by encouraging me and asking about my life. I always knew that Rev. Rita was a special person and pastor, but

CHAPTER 7

when I heard a story about her on the news, God affirmed that the time I had with her was a gift.

The NBC 12 News in Richmond, Virginia, reported on this amazing story.[7] Rev. Rita had recently been diagnosed with pancreatic cancer, and her husband was also ailing. In making end-of-life decisions and thinking she would be the first to pass away, Rita began the process of putting her husband in a care facility so that he would have the care he needed after her death. She also began the process of selling her house. Tragically, her husband died suddenly after a bad fall five days after he entered the care facility.

Rev. Rita still needed to sell her house and sell it quickly. As she was thinking about potential clients, she remembered fondly a conversation that she had had with one of her members many years ago. She decided to call Christine, a young woman whom she had pastored, a person who always loved her house. She had stayed in touch with Christine all this time and thought she had nothing to lose by reaching out to her. Christine and her husband were very excited that the house was for sale, and they said they would buy it on one condition . . . that Rita continue to live there with them.

So, the three became a family. Christine shared that she decided to ask Rita to stay to show her the same love that Rita had showed to her since she was eleven years old. This pastor, this recent widow, was able to live out her final days in the comfort of her home, all because Christine and her husband chose to make her a part of their family because they wanted to return the love that Rita had so freely given to them. This act truly embodies the servant ministry of Jesus Christ and Christian hospitality at its finest.

Jesus calls us to live in this kind of community—where we are obligated to each other, not out of fear or guilt but out of joy and love. As you wrestle with the obligations in your life, take some time to spend in community. Get to know the people around you. Practice

Christian hospitality, and thank God for everyone who has been entrusted to your care. Find a way to serve God in the way in which you are being called, and God will be with you.

PRAY

Wrestle with me, God, when I feel weighed down with obligation. Help me to see that obligation to you is a joy and not a burden. Wrestle with me, God, when I am distracted by the obligations in my life. Make a way forward for me to serve you. Amen.

REFLECT

1. Do you see some of yourself in Naomi and Ruth's story? If so, where?
2. What kinds of obligation hold people back from answering God's call?
3. Who is your "Ruth"? Who has been a friend who has stayed beside you?
4. Who invited you to be part of the family of Christ or made you feel welcomed? Who have you welcomed? What are some ways the church can be more welcoming?
5. How can you help others be enveloped in the care of their Christian community?

LISTEN

"Make Me a Servant" by the Maranatha Singers: https://www.youtube.com/watch?v=Y3vywgc2Tm4

JOURNAL

In what ways do you feel called to care for your community?

8
Wrestling with Letting Go
THE DISCIPLES

Now the eleven disciples went to Galilee, to the mountain to which Jesus had directed them. When they saw him, they worshiped him; but some doubted. And Jesus came and said to them, "All authority in heaven and on earth has been given to me. Go therefore and make disciples of all nations, baptizing them in the name of the Father and of the Son and of the Holy Spirit, and teaching them to obey everything that I have commanded you. And remember, I am with you always, to the end of the age." (Matt 28:16-20)

Changed Lives

This moment of commissioning changed the lives of every disciple present that day. Their mission was now clear. Their job in life was to continue the ministry of Jesus Christ to everyone they encountered. For the past three years the disciples had sacrificed everything to follow Jesus from place to place. They left their professions, homes, and families to follow the Son of God. In Christ they found a new identity, a new purpose for their lives, and a new understanding of their own calls. In Christ they found a blessing and a new way forward.

CHAPTER 8

In this moment of coming face-to-face with the risen Savior, some of the disciples believed, and some doubted. As we continue our journey of discernment, we will also experience seasons of trust and seasons of doubt. The beauty of the Great Commission is that our response to being called by God to serve should be worship. We worship God with our lives when we are ready to let go of life as we know it and open ourselves to the possibilities of a new life with Christ. We worship God with our lives when we attune ourselves more to God's will than to our own will. We worship God when we offer our entire selves and lives to God.

Take Nothing with You

Letting go could not have been easy for the disciples, and many of them wrestled with this newfound understanding of who Christ was calling them to be. Jesus called them to let go of everything familiar and follow him. In fact, the first time Jesus sent them out on their own, he told them: "Take nothing for your journey, no staff, nor bag, nor bread, nor money—not even an extra tunic. Whatever house you enter, stay there, and leave from there" (Luke 9:3-4). The disciples weren't able to take any kind of security blanket with them. The fishermen—Peter, Andrew, James, and John—who were used to taking everything they would need for a trip at sea, traded in their fishing nets for miracle stories. The tax collector, Matthew, traded his livelihood for the gift of community. Although the professions of some the disciples are unknown, they each traded in the familiar for the unknown. They had to leave their baggage, favorite snacks, and the security of money behind and completely put their trust in Jesus Christ. Above all, Jesus taught the disciples to continue to trust in God and to rely on the body of Christ.

In the moment of the Great Commission, Jesus was again calling the disciples to do something new. Earlier, Christ had given them authority to heal in his name; now he was giving them the authority to teach and preach the good news of Jesus Christ.[1] Like the prophets who had come before them, the disciples were now called to be the mouthpiece of God. They were being called to baptize and make disciples for Jesus Christ. With each person they would baptize, Christ charged them to say, "I baptize you 'in the name of the Father and of the Son and of the Holy Spirit'" (Matt 28:19). In this statement, they would remember that their ministry was not about them but about reminding people that God wanted to be in a relationship with them.

We use these same words of commissioning when we send people out into the mission field. We use these words because Christ's ministry in the world continues; Jesus is not finished with us or our world. Like the disciples, we do not do this ministry alone. Christ continues to lead us forward by the power of the Holy Spirit. We take heart in the fact that Jesus tasked an imperfect group of people to do this important work. After all, Jesus does not commission "angels or perfect believers, but the worshiping and wavering community of disciples."[2] Just when you think your imperfection takes you out of the running for ministry, think again. We, like the disciples, will have times in our lives when we wrestle with letting go.

In seminary I met a girl named Katie. She had a gnarly scar on her arm, and I knew she had a story to tell about it. Soon we became friends, and Katie shared with me how she got that scar. One summer, as she was further discerning her call while working at a camp, she had a major accident on a ropes course; she fell sixty feet and sustained life-threatening injuries. This was the first time Katie had ever wrestled with God. Everything had been going so well for her. This accident made her question God's presence in her life.

Katie was blessed to survive that accident and ended up spending her nineteenth birthday recovering at a nursing home. Like Jacob, Katie was determined she was not going to let go without her blessing. She did not lose her faith, a feat she attributes to God's grace. Later, Katie reflected that God was with her the whole time,

CHAPTER 8

just not in the way she expected. She said, "The cards and gifts that people sent and the visits that I received are where God's presence was made known to me."

Katie continued to discern God's call and eventually went to seminary. While in seminary, she started exhibiting some strange symptoms and learned that she had a brain tumor. Just when Katie thought she could put her health concerns behind her, she was going into the unknown again. A lot was unknown about the tumor, other than it could have been the reason for the epilepsy she had suffered since she was a teen, so it was determined that it needed to be removed. Again, Katie asked God, "Why?" She wondered if she should give up on her call. She clung to God, her faith community, and friends; and she made it through that difficult time. She recovered from her surgery, graduated seminary on time, and considers herself a "holy instigator" as she serves as the district vitality associate, helping churches in her district live out God's calling upon their lives in new and creative ways.

Katie is a constant source of hope and encouragement in my life. In her wrestling with God and letting go of her own timeline for the way she thought her life would go, I and countless others have been blessed by her ministry and her ever-present faith. Katie embodies a life of surrender and continues to be open to where God is calling her to go next.

When we say yes to God, we are called to let go of life as we know it and trust in God's plan for our lives. No matter what we may face, God will be there for us through it all, and God gives us the body of Christ to support and encourage us along the way. The prerequisite for disciple making is faith in Jesus Christ and the gifts of the Spirit, which will allow you to share the good news and care for the body of Christ. This ministry is not about us, but it is about the people we serve. We do not do this work in our own name but in the name of the Father, Son, and Holy Spirit.

Let Go of Fear

There may be many things that you are not ready to let go. Perhaps you are holding on to fear. Unlike Peter, you may be like the rest of the disciples out on the water that fateful day, not ready to get out of the boat and walk on the water. You may be afraid of what will happen once you surrender your life to God. The unknown may be keeping you awake at night. It is normal to experience some form of fear as you surrender your life to God, but you cannot let it entrap you. Instead, you can let this fear sharpen you and urge you to move forward.

What frightens you?

We know that Peter let his fear get the best of him on the day that someone asked him if he was a disciple of Christ. He denied Jesus not once but three times and was not at the crucifixion for Jesus's final moments. Fear kept Peter from Christ and from living into the person, the "rock" that Christ called him to be (Matt 16:18). Fear made the Israelites fashion a golden calf to worship. Fear made Jonah run the other way. Fear made Jacob flee from home, afraid for his very life. Fear made the disciples awaken Jesus on the boat when a storm came up. Fear is the robber of joy and the destroyer of futures. We are all afraid of something, but God calls us forward to serve anyway.

Let Go of Complacency

Perhaps it is complacency that you do not want to let go. You may be perfectly content with your life and not want to rock the boat. God does not call us to live comfortable lives; in fact, ministry is often uncomfortable and even awkward. If you never go beyond your comfort zone, you cannot truly answer God's call. The most powerful evangelists of our time are those who are willing to travel around the world to tell others how God has changed their lives. In complacency there is no wrestling with God. If you are not intentional about wrestling with God, then change cannot occur.

What Are You Looking For?

I have always been in awe of the call story of the first disciples in John 1. Jesus's baptism impacted John the Baptist greatly and gave him even more passion to share the good news of Jesus Christ. One particular day, as John was speaking about Jesus to anyone who would listen, two of John's disciples took notice and wanted to know more. So they followed Jesus, and he turned to them and asked, "What are you looking for?" (John 1:38). What a great question from Jesus!

We are all looking for something, aren't we? Whether we look for acceptance, a way forward, peace, joy, or love—we are all on a journey. Andrew and Peter recognized that they had come across someone special, and they felt it. In their spirit they already felt that they needed to follow this person, so they asked Jesus where he was staying. Jesus replied, "Come and see" (v. 39). This was not simply an invitation to see Jesus's accommodations; it was a call to discipleship. Then the most amazing thing happened; the two men listened to Jesus's invitation and followed him.

> What are you looking for? In a job? In a relationship? In your faith?

Right before the Great Commission passage, we read the words, "come" and "see" again (Matt 28:6). This time they are not uttered by Jesus but by an angel of the Lord who showed the women who came to the tomb that Jesus was not there. Every day, Christ calls us to come and see the ministry to which we have been called, but sometimes we do not heed Christ's invitation. We make excuses and say, "Maybe later, Lord." Sometimes we can't let go of distractions due to the possibility of denominational differences or the sad events in the world, and we stop looking for Jesus Christ. Sometimes we feel that we are not ready to answer God's call. Other times, pride or fear stops us from answering God's call. The same Peter who heeded Christ's call to "come and see" was the one who denied him three times in his greatest time of need. But God was not finished with Peter. Peter claimed his call on the Day of Pentecost when he preached a powerful sermon and about three thousand people were baptized (Acts 2:41).

Waiting on the Holy Spirit

Just as the disciples waited fifty days for the coming of the Holy Spirit, we also must wait for guidance from the Holy Spirit about our next steps on this journey of discernment. We must realize that God cannot be put in a box and that God answers on God's timeline, not ours. Be patient; discerning God's call on your life may take some time. Be determined, as you will need to put in the time, work, study, and prayers while you continue to answer God's call on your life. God's call can change over time. Be open to the infinite possibilities of where God may call you to serve, and find people who support and celebrate your call. In the meantime, look for what God is already doing in your life. Be in mission and ministry where you are.

Called to New Life

One of my favorite illustrations of new life is the process of a caterpillar becoming a butterfly. A couple years ago, I heard a sermon by my friend and colleague Rev. Meredith McNabb, who completely shattered my understanding of how this amazing event occurs. Up until that point, I had always thought that when the caterpillar entered the cocoon or chrysalis, it just received some new wings and became a butterfly. My friend Meredith shared that while in the cocoon, the caterpillar—now in the pupa stage—begins to digest itself, turning itself into caterpillar soup.

I find it amazing that within the broken-down caterpillar soup are a few "imaginal discs" for each body part needed for the butterfly.[3]

Some parts of the caterpillar are still preserved to be combined with these new cells to make a butterfly. It really is a blending of the old and the new. Dr. Lincoln Brower explains, "Literally the entire internal contents of the caterpillar—the muscles, the entire digestive system, even the heart, even the nervous system—is totally rebuilt."[4] You see, when the caterpillar is in the chrysalis, it must die to life the way it was lived before so that new life can spring forth. Yet, hidden in the chrysalis is the promise of new life from only a couple of cells ... this process is truly a miracle.

God also calls us to this new life through surrender. Here is our life song: God calls, we surrender, and God works through us for God's glory. The disciples surrendered their livelihoods, being with family, the comforts of their homes, their pride, their whole selves, to the work of Christ. Are you ready to take a step of faith and surrender your whole life to God?

Cutting everything loose is scary, isn't it? I still have butterflies of anxiety in my belly when God calls me to do something new, yet this is what God does. God continues to call us out of our comfort zones to sing "a new song" all for God's glory (Ps 96:1). Answering God's calling upon your life can be scary, but it is also freeing. It is a chance to move forward into God's preferred future for us individually and corporately as a community of faith. God's call frees us for joyful obedience, to be the hands and feet of Christ.

In Mission Together

When you set off on a mission for the Lord, it is easy to feel as if you are a hero coming to save the day. But as Rev. Dr. Denise Honeycutt, the past director of the United Methodist Committee on Relief (UMCOR), has taught me, we are in mission *with* people, not *to* them. Mission and ministry are reciprocal, and each person participating in God's holy work has equal standing at Christ's Communion table.

Over the course of her ministry, Denise has followed Christ to the many different places where Christ has called her to go. She has shared her passion for mission at the local church, conference, and global levels, and the way she ignites this passion in others is through connecting them. One thing Denise realized when she served a large church was that people didn't know each other. She decided quickly to do a sermon series highlighting the gifts of many people in her congregation. Denise told her congregation, "God can call and use anyone no matter what vocation they choose. God is already using you, and we need to name it and claim it."

We must let go of what we think mission should be as we open our eyes to see what God is already doing in the present. Just as Christ called the disciples in that moment to serve, God calls us every moment of every day to embody our inward faith into outward mission and service. God's work is never what we expect; it is better because in these unforeseen situations we are free to venture out and see more clearly how God is working with us and, sometimes, despite us. Mission and ministry go hand in hand; you cannot have one without the other. In ministry we are formed in discipleship then sent out into the world, beyond the walls of the church to do mission. God is always calling us to do unexpected things, but we do not do them alone. God is with us, leading us forward as we stand beside the body of Christ.

When Jesus was crucified, the disciples' world turned upside down, and they were afraid they were next. They had left everything to follow Jesus. Yes, there was betrayal, denial, and failure; but from the disciples' point of view, they had been through a lot. Now there were rumors of a resurrection. They must have believed, at least to some extent, the words of the women at the tomb; that is, that an angel directed the disciples to go to Galilee where Jesus would meet them. But there were other rumors that some disciples had stolen Jesus's body and were propagating the far-fetched story that he had come back to life or perhaps he never did die. What should they do?

Fortunately for them, and us, the disciples went to the appointed mountain in Galilee to see for themselves, and they indeed met Jesus, who then commissioned them. He wasn't finished with them; there was a lot more to do. Similarly, as Moses received the Ten Commandments on Mount Sanai to instruct God's people in discipleship, the disciples received Christ's authority to carry on the ministry of Jesus Christ. But they wouldn't go alone. Jesus would go with them through the Holy Spirit.

You are also invited to come and see. You are invited to leave behind your fear and anxiety, your past and preconceptions, your failures—perhaps even your plans—and walk confidently into the future to do God's work in the name of the Father, Son, and Holy Spirit. God has been with you. God is with you. God will be with you.

My hope is that this study has helped you discern further the way in which God is calling you to serve. But know this: you will always have opportunities to serve, whether you are volunteer or doing professional mission and ministry. No matter how you serve, always let go and know that God and the body of Christ go with you.

The Wrestling Goes On

Even after you surrender your life to God, you will continue to wrestle with God. You will experience this blessed wrestling throughout the rest of your life because this is how the Holy Spirit will alert you to injustice, to those who need grace, to changes you need to make in your own life, and how best to use your gifts. Wrestling with letting go does not just happen the moment before you surrender your life to God. It happens every day, over and over again. It can happen at each new church you serve or each new place you go. Letting go happens throughout the course of your discipleship. You must be willing to let go to receive all that God has in store for you.

You never know when and where God will call you to let go. You must be on the lookout for God. You must open your heart to the movement of the Holy Spirit. One of these "come and see" moments happened to me when I attended my annual conference. One of my favorite moments each year at the Virginia Conference of The United Methodist Church happens during the service of the ordering of ministry. This is the moment that pastors are licensed, commissioned, and ordained by the bishop. These moments are important, as people who have been working for many years to become pastors finally find themselves living into these roles. Yet, often, the most impactful part of the service happens at the end when the bishop issues a call to all who are in attendance.

The bishop says, "I now invite anyone who feels called to ministry and mission to come forward and receive prayer." Music starts playing. At first no one walks to the front of the room; then, one by one, people start coming. They start off coming alone, but then start coming in groups. People who are young and old, and even children, walk to the front to pray with the bishop. It is a very impactful service as the Holy Spirit moves.

Twenty years ago I found myself in one of these services knowing I was called to be a pastor but not yet ready to let others know. In a way I wanted to go forward, but I was not ready to let go. Have you ever been in that situation? Maybe you have been in a church service when the pastor has asked for help with a specific task, and you think to yourself, "I would really like to do that." Then for whatever reason, you never follow up with the pastor. Sometimes we feel that we aren't ready or that someone else may be able to do a better job. Just remember that the tugging on your heart to serve is from the Holy Spirit.

For me, in the moment the bishop made the call to come forward, the Holy Spirit was yelling, "Go!" But I could not get myself to move. Then suddenly my friend Lynda pulled me out of my row and said, "Jessie, it's time to go." I knew what she meant, so I followed her, and hand in hand we walked toward the bishop. Lynda and I were an unlikely pair as we walked up the aisle. I was a sixteen-year-old Caucasian teenager, and she was a middle-aged, African

CHAPTER 8

American woman who was an ordained minister in a Baptist church. Lynda saw something in me that I was not ready to see in myself. I knew I was called, but I didn't know what to do next. Lynda provided that opportunity for me as she listened to the Holy Spirit. I often wonder where I would be now if Lynda had not invited me to take that important walk that day. I think this is why I am so passionate about helping others to discern God's call. I don't want anyone to miss out on what God is calling them to do.

Next Steps

You may be able to relate to my experience at the annual conference. You feel called to mission or ministry, but you don't know your next steps. To you, I recommend further discernment. The early church had it right; the way you can continue to know God and God's will for your life is by reading the Bible, spending time in fellowship with the body of Christ, and prayer (Acts 2:42). Also, talking with a trusted mentor, pastor, or friend is key. The conversation with one of these people may be the nudge you need to finally move forward and answer God's call.

As I walked toward the bishop that day, I knew this was another pivotal moment for me in my journey to the ministry. It was my moment of public declaration that I had been called to ministry and that I was going to do something about it. I saw knowing smiles as I walked down the long aisle to the bishop. Some people I knew even had tears in their eyes, as this was a moment of confirmation for them that I had been called. I share with you this important story in my life because sometimes it takes other people to help us answer God's call. God has given us the gift of the church; together we are called to make disciples for God's glory. Today, Lynda and I are both United Methodist pastors, and we serve on the Board of Ordained Ministry together.

So, when you wrestle with God, do not despair; but look for the blessing. Meditate upon what God is asking you to do or where

God is asking you to go. Confess your spiritual wrestling matches to those you love, and you may be surprised by the experiences they have to share with you. Through wrestling with God, you will be blessed and sent forward with hope. My hope is that you now see a next step forward, no matter how small it may be. Every person God has called started by taking one step at a time.

Wrestling with Letting Go Spotlight: Bishop John Yambasu

A spiritual giant in the world of United Methodism was Bishop John Yambasu. Before his tragic death in a car crash in August of 2020, Bishop Yambasu was the resident bishop of Sierra Leone, the president of the United Methodist Africa College of Bishops, and the chancellor of Africa University. Bishop Yambasu was known for his passion for mission, his advocacy for children, and his ability to bring diverse groups of people together to move forward in unity. One of the most amazing things that God called Bishop Yambasu to do was to start the Child Rescue Centre in Sierra Leone.

The Helping Children Worldwide web site states, "On July 4, 2000 the Child Rescue Centre was founded in the city of Bo, Sierra Leone. From those first 40 children, the Child Rescue Centre (CRC) has grown to include a spectrum of programs serving more than 600 extremely vulnerable children and youth, helping them escape the vicious cycle of poverty and develop their full potential."[5] Through the relationships that Bishop Yambasu built with others he was able to do so much Kingdom building in his lifetime. One of these relationships was with Floris United Methodist Church in Virginia. Bishop Yambasu partnered with this church in mission and soon developed a deep friendship with their pastor, Rev. Tom Berlin.

In a tribute to the bishop, Tom described Bishop Yambasu's gifts for Kingdom building: "Bishop Yambasu was a remarkable leader who built international ministry partnerships across the United States and Europe."[6] Wherever he went, Bishop Yambasu carried an

CHAPTER 8

infectious faith and the hope that we all could be better Christians if we helped one another.

I was blessed to serve on the General Board of Global Ministries with Bishop Yambasu. I always looked forward to his powerful sermons and prayers. He spoke so passionately about Jesus Christ, but there was always a gentleness to him. He felt compelled to bring people together from all over the world in the name of Jesus. Recently, in a press release from UMCMission.org, Thomas Kemper, the former general secretary of the General Board of Global Ministries, described Bishop Yambasu's impact on his life and the world: "He was the voice for health, justice and peace in all matters sacred and secular. . . . His lifelong experience in the church . . . prepared him for outstanding leadership across boundaries."[7]

Bishop Yambasu traveled all over the world preaching the good news of Jesus Christ, and his legacy will live on through all of us who were blessed to know him and work alongside him. He let go of the comforts of his home to go and be with God's people and instruct them to live out the Great Commission.

You are also called to go and make disciples of all nations by saying yes to God. My prayer is that you have found greater clarity in discernment through studying the call stories of the Bible and hearing the call stories of so many different people. May you be changed and blessed wherever God is leading you, and may you never forget we always go forward with hope!

PRAY

Wrestle with me, God, and propel me forward by the power of your Holy Spirit to answer your calling upon my life. Wrestle with me when I try to control your work in a world that is uncontrollable.

Help me to let go of my pride, fear, and anything else that is getting in the way of my saying yes to you. Amen.

REFLECT

1. How might Christ be calling you to come and see?
2. Are you hearing God's call to professional ministry or mission?
3. What are your next steps? Do you need to speak with someone?
4. What do you need to let go of in order to answer God's call?
5. Where will you continue to find support in your journey of discernment?

LISTEN

"Spirit Lead Me" by Michael Ketterer and Influence Music
https://www.youtube.com/watch?v=ABWnLjXer10

JOURNAL

How is God calling you to build up the kingdom of God on earth?

Afterword: Next Steps

So, YOU FEEL CALLED. Now what? I am so thankful you have taken time to wrestle with God and discern God's call upon your life. I pray you have found some clarity through this process and that you have some next steps to take as you continue to answer God's call. If you are looking for some continued ways to discern, check out the opportunities below:

1. Talk to your pastor if you are connected to a church, and share with them where you are in your discernment process. If you do not have a church home, seek one out and become a member so that you can continue your discernment with a loving community to support you.
2. Try out a facet of ministry or mission that interests you. Maybe this involves shadowing a pastor, preaching, teaching Sunday school, or going on a mission trip. By trying out the things you are interested in, you will be able to discern if that is where God is calling you to be.
3. Plan for the long-term and not the short-term; answering God's call is a lifelong process. Give yourself some grace. Find out the process for the ministry or mission to which you have been called. These processes can be long, but take it one step at a time.

4. Find others to hold you accountable and pray with you as you answer God's call. Whether this is a trusted friend, pastor, family member, or mentor, having someone ask about your progress is very helpful.
5. Practice spiritual disciplines like reading Scripture or participating in a Bible study. Find a prayer partner or an accountability partner with whom you can share openly. Practice fasting from food, or take a fast from social media for a certain period. Spend time in prayer each day wrestling with God as you further discern God's call.
6. Get to know yourself better, and practice holistic self-care. The better you know yourself, the better you can share the good news of Christ with others. Take one of the assessments mentioned in chapter 5 and talk over your results with someone who really knows you. Share what surprised you and what you already know to be true. Make sure that you are keeping a day of sabbath each week so that you can rest and find renewal.
7. Get involved in your community. This is how you start practicing ministry and mission where you are. Volunteer for community events so that you can learn about and respond to the needs of your community.
8. Do not give up. God will continue to lead you forward with hope!

Commissioning Prayer and Blessing

Sending God, send us out, individually or together. Send us to the places that are hurting and that need Christ's healing. Send us to places where we would not go on our own. Continue to reveal to us the ways in which we can continue to respond to your call, and use our gifts to build up the body of Christ. Send us forth in joy and with hope, we pray. Amen.

Notes

CHAPTER 1

1. Leander Keck, ed., *The New Interpreter's Bible Commentary*, vol. 1 (Nashville: Abingdon Press, 1994), 565.
2. Keck, 565.
3. Leander E. Keck, ed., *The New Interpreter's Bible Commentary*, vol. 1 (Nashville: Abingdon Press, 2015), 202.
4. Katharine Doob Sakenfeld, ed., *The New Interpreter's Dictionary of the Bible*, vol. 4 (Nashville: Abingdon Press, 2009), 440.
5. St. Augustine, *Confessions*, trans. and ed. Albert C. Outler (Philadelphia: Westminster Press, 1955), accessed August 10, 2021, https://www.ling.upenn.edu/courses/hum100/augustinconf.pdf.

CHAPTER 2

1. *The HarperCollins Study Bible*, New Revised Standard Version (New York: HarperCollins, 1993), 1011.
2. *HarperCollins Study Bible*, 1022.
3. Matthew Skinner, *Acts: Catching Up with the Spirit* (Nashville: Abingdon Press, 2020), 15.
4. Rachel Billups, *Be Bold: Finding Your Fierce* (Nashville: Abingdon Press, 2019), 2–4.
5. Rachel Billups, *Be Bold: Finding Your Fierce* Promo Video, June 4, 2019, https://www.youtube.com/watch?v=sZHmQl_DSm8.

6. "Social Principles: The Nurturing Community," from *The Book of Discipline of The United Methodist Church* (2016), UMC.org, https://www.umc.org/en/content/social-principles-the-nurturing-community#human-sexuality.

CHAPTER 3

1. Leander E. Keck, ed., *The New Interpreter's Bible Commentary*, vol. 8 (Nashville: Abingdon Press, 2015), 39.
2. Patricia Chadwick, "Mary Mother of Jesus," *History's Women*, accessed August 10, 2021, http://www.historyswomen.com/womenoffaith/mary.htm.
3. Chadwick.
4. Mark Wilson, "Were Mary and Joseph Married or Engaged at Jesus' Birth?" *Bible History Daily*, Biblical Archaeology Society, accessed July 14, 2021, https://www.biblicalarchaeology.org/daily/biblical-topics/bibleinterpretation/were-mary-and-joseph-married-or-engaged-at-jesus-birth/.
5. Chadwick, "Mary Mother of Jesus."
6. Adam Hamilton, *Final Words from the Cross* (Nashville: Abingdon Press, 2011), 54–55.
7. Keck, *New Interpreter's Bible Commentary*, vol. 2, 718.

CHAPTER 4

1. Katherine Doob Sakenfeld, ed., *The New Interpreter's Dictionary of the Bible*, vol. 4 (Nashville: Abingdon Press, 2007), 407.
2. Brené Brown, "The Power of Vulnerability," Ted Talk (June 2010), https://www.ted.com/talks/brene_brown_on_vulnerability?language=en.
3. "Why Did God Change Saul's Name to Paul?" *Catholic Answers*, accessed July 26, 2021, https://www.catholic.com/qa/why-did-god-change-sauls-name-to-paul.
4. "Services for the Ordering of Ministry in The United Methodist Church, 2017–2020," accessed November 18, 2016, https://www.umcdiscipleship.org/resources/services-for-ordering-of-ministry-in-the-united-methodist-church-2017-2020.

CHAPTER 5

1. Irene Nowell, *Women in the Old Testament* (Collegeville, MN: Liturgical Press, 1997), 64.
2. "The Baptismal Covenant I," *The United Methodist Hymnal* (Nashville: The United Methodist Publishing House, 1989), 34.

3. "Introduction to the Eight Concepts," The Bowen Center for the Study of the Family, accessed July 26, 2021, https://www.thebowencenter.org/introduction-eight-concepts.
4. "Everyday Disciples: John Wesley's 22 Questions," *Discipleship Ministries of The United Methodist Church*, accessed October 25, 2016, https://www.umcdiscipleship.org/resources/everyday-disciples-john-wesleys-22-questions.
5. *The Wesley Study Bible*, New Revised Standard Version (Nashville: Abingdon, 2009), 302.

CHAPTER 6

1. Katharine Doob Sakenfeld, ed., *The New Interpreter's Dictionary of the Bible*, vol. 2 (Nashville: Abingdon Press, 2007), 317.
2. Douglas Main, "Murder Hornets Have Arrived in the U.S.—Here's What You Should Know," *National Geographic*, (May 4, 2020), https://www.nationalgeographic.com/animals/2020/05/asian-giant-hornets-arrive-united-states/#:~:text=Update%20on%20May%2029%2C%202020,that%20it%20produced%20many%20queens.
3. Albert C. Outler and Richard P. Heitzenrater, "The Circumcision of the Heart," *John Wesley's Sermons: An Anthology* (Nashville: Abingdon Press, 1991), 23.
4. *The Book of Discipline of The United Methodist Church* (Nashville: The United Methodist Publishing House, 2016), ¶104, §3, 74.
5. Sakenfeld, *New Interpreter's Dictionary of the Bible*, vol. 2, 317.

CHAPTER 7

1. Leonard E. Keck, ed., *The New Interpreter's Bible Commentary*, vol. 2 (Nashville: Abingdon Press, 2015), 274.
2. Stanley Hauerwas, quoted in William Willimon, *Pastor: The Theology and Practice of Ordained Ministry*, rev. ed. (Nashville: Abingdon Press, 2016), 60.
3. David Lowes Watson, *The Early Methodist Class Meeting* (Nashville: Discipleship Resources, 1985), 93.
4. "Everyday Disciples: John Wesley's 22 Questions," *Discipleship Ministries of The United Methodist Church*, accessed October 25, 2016, https://www.umcdiscipleship.org/resources/everyday-disciples-john-wesleys-22-questions.
5. "The Baptismal Covenant I," *The United Methodist Hymnal*, (Nashville: The United Methodist Publishing House, 1989), 15.

6. Katherine Doob Sakenfeld, ed., *The New Interpreter's Dictionary of the Bible*, vol. 4 (Nashville: Abingdon Press, 2007), 865.
7. Anthony Antoine, "Acts of Kindness: Richmond Couple Takes in Ailing Minister," *NBC 12 News Richmond*, (September 4, 2018), https://www.nbc12.com/story/39023929/richmond-couple-takes-in-ailing-minister/.

CHAPTER 8

1. Leander E. Keck, ed., *The New Interpreter's Bible Commentary*, vol. 7 (Nashville: Abingdon Press, 2015), 376.
2. Keck, 375.
3. Ferris Jabr, "How Does a Caterpillar Turn into a Butterfly?" *Scientific American* (August 10, 2012), https://www.scientificamerican.com/article/caterpillar-butterfly-metamorphosis-explainer/.
4. Dr. Lincoln Brower, "Inside the Chrysalis," *Journey North*, accessed July 23, 2021, https://journeynorth.org/tm/monarch/ChrysalisDevelopmentLPB.html.
5. "Our Story," *Helping Children Worldwide*, accessed August 1, 2020, https://www.helpingchildrenworldwide.org/our-story.html.
6. Rev. Tom Berlin, "A Tribute to Bishop John K. Yambasu," *RevTomBerlin.com*, accessed August 24, 2020, https://revtomberlin.com/a-tribute-to-bishop-john-k-yambasu/?fbclid=IwAR2YTQ9R7Btc8pF5ME2U-0Sa9076fI3m5XDSSdmkzQsIE-doBwDT8GGOfow.
7. Thomas Kemper, "Remembering Bishop John Yambasu," *Global Ministries of The United Methodist Church*, accessed August 17, 2020, https://www.umcmission.org/share-our-work/news-stories/2020/press-release-and-statements-2020/remembering-bishop-john-yambasu.

Free videos, graphics, and sermon series information are available for this study at www.blessedwrestling.com.

www.ingramcontent.com/pod-product-compliance
Lightning Source LLC
Chambersburg PA
CBHW010045090426
42735CB00020B/3397